Mealthy CrispLid
Cookbook for Beginners

Amazingly Easy and Delicious Recipes to Fry, Grill and Roast
with the Mealthy CrispLid for Any Pressure Cooker

By Emily Rose

Table of Content

Introduction

I have always wanted my food to be crispy and crunchy in every bite. And the sound that it makes when I chew the food is what makes me go crazy. I have been cooking with the instant pot earlier, and my electric cooker also works like a wondrous cooking machine. So, I guess I had no inherent motive to buy a new and advanced Mealthy Crisplid just to check it out how it works and how it is different.

But I got an opportunity to review the new Mealthy Pot, and I have to say that it was good that the good guys at Mealthy chose me to check it out. Otherwise, I would have never gone out just to buy it. I wouldn't have, it is true.

It was because of my expertise in the cooking industry that I got a chance to use it for free and share my experience. To my surprise, the Crisplid turned out to be a fantastic product that had everything that I needed to make my food crispier than ever.

Chapter 1 The Crazy Mealthy Crisplid

What is Mealthy Crisplid?

My answer to this question is simply that this is an add-on device that can be attached to your pressure cooker so that it starts working as an air-fryer. Now the question which arises is why an Air-Fryer?

And I am guessing that you know about an air fryer and how it helps to prepare your food. A Mealthy pot is the next best thing that you can get after the instant pot. It cooks beautifully, does not harm the integrity of the dish, and uses only the required amount of oil to turn your normal food into ambrosia. Yes, it can do that, provided you know how to use it.

And that is my motive of writing this book, to tell you how to use the Mealthy Crisplid so that the next time you use, the food won't turn out soggy or undercooked. Because a lot of people complain about this aspect when they use an air fryer. Plus, I want you to know how best to use the lid for preparing your food and what all you can cook in it. And don't worry, you will get a big list of recipes along with their preparation method in the book. So, sit tight because you are in for a fantastic ride.

So, this begs the question, why not use an air fryer? Well, the answer is simple. With an air fryer, I cannot see my food see my being transformed. I mean, the very first thing that I cooked in it was potatoes. I wanted to start with something simple. And fried potatoes were the first thing that came to my mind. And they turned out to be amazing and perfect. So, I guess this was a good start.

The Special Functions of Mealthy Crisplid

Is there something special about the mechanics of this lid?

Hmmmmm….. Yes, there is. The main motive of using this Crisplid is to make your food lighter. Lighter in the sense that you won't feel a burden before or after eating and especially won't have to deal with a heavy stomach. This is because the heating system is developed to give the right amount of heat and precision cooking with fewer amount of oils.

Taking too much of oils that will increase the fats. But, that won't be an issue once you get the Mealthy Crisplid. And it is not that you will have to spend a fortune on this small add-on to your pressure cooker. Nah! It won't even pinch your pocket. But the benefits entailed with it are numerous.

On top of the lid, you will notice some controls which will help you navigate through the whole system and cook some exquisite cuisines within minutes. The heating panel is situated on the bottom side, and on top of it, you have the control panel. The glass lid will provide you with a clear view of the food being cooked, baked, broiled, or crisped.

This is how it all goes down. You will set the timer as per the dish, and then the heat will be distributed throughout the whole electric cooker or the pot. This ensures that your dish is getting just the right amount of heat for it to be prepared with perfection.

You can use the single lid to cover both types of electric cooker 6 quartz or the 8 quartz. Added to this, the Mealthy Crisplid is also fully compatible with the Mealthy Pot.

More importantly, when you are using the Mealthy Crisp lid, there is no need to plug the electric cooker or the instant pot. This small appliance does all the work that is done by any instant pot only with less power consumption. Along with this, there is less usage of oil, and still, you will get better food quality and finish. Where else can you get that?

The Benefits of Using Mealthy Crisplid:

There is a lot to talk about this part. The Mealthy Crisplid may not look like much, but it has some fantastic benefits. To start with, think of all the space that you are going to save, keeping this lid instead of buying a new air fryer. I have always wanted to know what happens inside a pressure cooker when my food is being cooked.

It's a good thing that I can see it now. Not only this, the crisp lid can turn your everyday electric cooker into a grill or even an oven. I have been checking a new trend in the diet of the millennials. The guys and gals who are into college or have recently come out of it tend to be more conscious of their health. They want food that is more conducive to their future health.

Moreover, their way of living and accommodative preferences are also different. That is why a Crisplid for them is the perfect appliance to take care of their health. They can eat good food and that too without compromising on the overall diet schedule.

And when it comes to preparing food, apart from air frying it, you can also use the Crisplid for broiling or making sure that the food is crispier and tastier. Browning your food with the help of a Crisplid is even better and a safer method.

I have been using this custom made air fryer for some time now. I have it almost when it was launched, and the company had sent me one for a test run. Ever since that day, there is a crisp lid in my kitchen all clean and tidy to help me prepare my food.

It is a bit inconvenient first to broil some dishes in the instant pot and then do the same in an oven. Instant pots do not go over 400° Celsius temperature. Whereas, this crisp lid can go up to 500°C, and this makes your work easier and faster.

All of this means that you will be working with a versatile appliance. Imagine first you are pressure cooking your food, then you are transferring it to an oven, and some of you may even put it on a grill. All of this will take time, effort, and not to mention the exposure to heat and burns.

The Mealthy Crisplid does make One Pot meals reality, and I would like to call it a wondrous experience.

Talking about the price aspect of this optimal appliance. Just now, we were talking about what all it can do. Now imagine spending money on all the appliances that are made to perform these tasks. You will need a separate oven, pressure cooker, instant pot, or even a grill and not to mention the cooktop.

This appliance will do all of this at a small cost of an instant pot and the Mealthy Crisplid itself.

Washing the pans and dishes that you may use for cooking with all the other appliances and utensils will only add to your work. Because the Crisplid can perform various tasks at once, there will be fewer pans and, consequently, less work for you after preparing the food.

And cleaning it is also not a big task. The glass lid can be scraped off with a soft cloth and just remove the splatters. All the other parts of the crisp lid like the mesh, trivet, silicon trivet, tongs, among others, are only small parts, and they can be washed in a dishwasher too. So, everything with the Mealthy Crisplid is super convenient.

Remember how you have to preheat the ovens or a standard air fryer before you can prepare anything in them. Well, to everyone's surprise, this is not the case with the Crisplid. I have heard a lot of men and women both complain about preheating. And sometimes, there are differences in the amount of heat supplied, which makes the whole dish vulnerable.

So, I guess it is a good thing that with the Mealthy Crisplid, there is no need to preheat the instant pot or the electric cooker. Just plug it in, put in the food, and you are good to go.

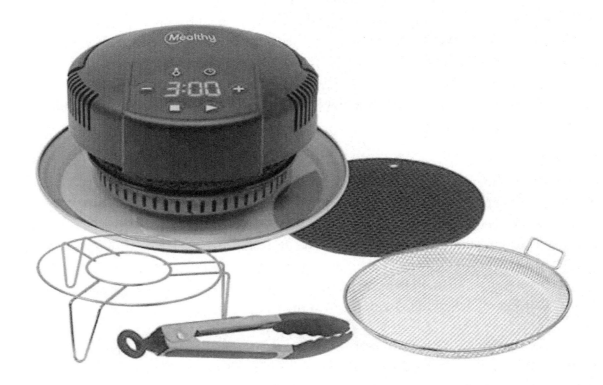

Using the Mealthy CrispLid

Using the crisp lid is as simple as it gets. The only thing that you need to do is attach it to the instant pot and then let the magic happen. Let me tell you about the different parts of your crisp lid.

The very first thing that you will notice is that the crisp lid has various parts. Take them all out and spread them on the table. Moving forward, it will get a bit technical, but it is also essential for you to understand how to use your Mealthy crisp lid for best results.

Let's start with the central unit, which has the main heating unit. This unit is operated by the control panel. The Mealthy Crisplid control panel is made simple for an everyday user, and it does not take much effort to get it working initially.

To use the crisp lid, make sure that you have unplugged your electric pressure cooker. The surface has to be flat and solid. Also, during operation, the crisp lid will get hot, so make sure that it is at an appropriate height where kids cannot reach.

There is a fryer basket that comes along with the crisp lid. You need to set the basket on the trivet. The trivet is kept inside the electric cooker steel pot. The motive is to make sure that the food items do not touch the surface of the steel pot directly. That it is always at a certain height.

The placement of trivet is even more critical when you are cooking larger food items. For small items like soups and other dishes that require minimum work, you can make them directly in the steel pot. Like a vegetable broil soup can be easily prepared in the crisp lid, and the way it is cooked is just excellent.

A vegetable broil was the first thing that I made with the crisp lid. And everybody thought that I had used a different recipe or added some secret sauce to make it tasty. That is the importance of preparing your food with the right heat and pressure.

It is a common practice that you have to flip the food under preparation after some time. In other electric cookers that I have used, even if I set the timer and temperature, it will all go back to default. But not with the crisp lid, with this, if you flip the food to make sure that it is cooking evenly from all sides, the timer and temperature won't turn back to default settings. This may not look like much of a feature in the book. But those who deal with this kind of issue every day will know the importance of this memory function.

The crisp lid glass is there to help those individuals who are very eager to check on their food every now and then. The truth is that this will lead to improper cooking of the food, and it won't taste as good as you imagined.

That is why the good guys at Mealthy have provided a glass lid so that you can see the food cooking in real-time.

I think that Mealthy CrispLid is a big help for everyone who is looking to follow a controlled diet. With other cooking methods, oil is an essential ingredient. It is needed for a whole lot of tasks. With the coming of air fryers, the usage of oil can be inhibited, but you will then need to buy an entirely new appliance.

Come the Mealthy Crisplid; you won't have to deal with the extra space and still get the same benefits that you can get with an air fryer.

I think that there are a lot of problems that crisp lid aims to solve. Be it preparing the food with a minimal amount of oil. Other than this, you can make sure that the food is properly cooked by observing it through the glass lid.

Safety is the Best Cure:

There are a few safety precautions that you will have to follow while working on the CrispLid. The most important reason is that the Crisplid works with heat, and it runs with electricity. So, always make sure that you follow the safety precautions given below:

- You are provided with a pair of tongs; it is best if you would use them to pick up the basket. Also, you can use the tongs to flip the food, but it is not so convenient and safe. The best practice is to pick the mesh basket with the tongs and keep it on the trivet or the silicone trivet. Flip the food and then place it back with the same set of tongs.
- Some foods do require you to heat it at temperatures above 450° Celsius. At this temperature, things get too hot to be controlled. So, if your Mealthy Crisplid turns off after 20 minutes of operating at this temperature, don't think that it is damaged. It is a safety feature embedded in the appliance. The important thing is that you need to wait for at least 10 minutes before you turn it on again.
- Do not place the Crisp lid on the kitchen shelf or any other non-heat resistant surface. It may damage the lid and the surface itself.
- The inner pot of your pressure cooker or the instant has the maximum extent up to which you can keep the food. When working with the Mealthy CrispLid, it is essential that your food always sits below this level.
- I guess this is evident, but let me warn you nonetheless. Never touch the out surface of the Crisplid. And this goes for every inch of the crisp lid but the handle. The handle is strategically located and covered to make sure that it does not get hot. If you want to remove the lid, lift it up from the handle only and nothing else.

- The inner pot is also hot, so take care while handling it. You can use oven mitts to remove it from the electric cooker or the instant pot.
- Understand that the crisp lid and the electric cooker that you use are two different things. So, when you are using either of them, do not plug in the other appliance. Basically, when you are using the Mealthy CrispLid, always make sure that the instant pot or the pressure cooker is not plugged in.

So, For Whom is This Book Perfect?

Well, I would say that this book is perfect for everybody. This is because day by day we are getting less and less time to eat healthily. So, an appliance which can help us speed up things and eat tastier food than ever before has to be there in your kitchen.

More than this, the Mealthy Crisp Lid will save you some money and space as it can be fitted with your current instant pot or pressure cooker and turn them into an air fryer.

So, basically, we will be getting a fantastic air fryer in your hands. And those who want to explore what an air fryer can do, just go for the Mealthy Crisplid.

Some questions that you may have:

U p until now, you may have figured out that this book will help you set up and use your Mealthy CrispLid efficiently. In the last part of the introduction, I will talk about some questions that you may have and answer them.

- **When Should I start cleaning the Crisplid?**

Well, you need to wait until and unless the Crisplid is cooled down. You cannot clean it when it is still hot. Be safe and protect your skin from heat damage.

- **Can I wash the Mealthy Crisplid parts in the Dishwasher?**

Yes, you can easily wash all the parts of the crisp lid in a dishwasher. For the glass lid, you can clean it with a damp cloth and make sure that all the food splatters are removed.

- **Why do the Mealthy Crisplid stops working when the heat reaches above 450°C?**

This has to do with overheating the food and also protecting the glass lid from excessive heat. Also, if you are using an instant pot made of any other material than steel, such high temperatures will lead to the shedding of chemicals from that material.

- **Does the Mealthy Crisplid come with a Warranty?**

Well, of course. You will get a limited one-year warranty.

Thank you for reading through the whole introduction part. I know you have been waiting to check out all the recipes that you can prepare in the Mealthy Crisplid. The next part is where you will find up to 80 different recipes that you can make in the Crisplid. I have added the ingredients needed to prepare every dish. Along with this, I have shared nutritional information for those who like to keep a count of their calories.

Chapter 2 Breakfast and Brunch

French Toast Sticks

Prep time: 5 minutes, Cook time: 10 minutes; Serves 2

Ingredients

2 slices whole grain/sprouted grain bread

1 egg

3 tablespoons unsweetened almond milk/milk of your choice

4 tsp maple syrup

½ tsp cinnamon

½ tsp vanilla extract

olive oil spray

Instructions

1. Line bottom of your instant pot with parchment paper. It prevents sticking.

2. Slice the bread into 4 equal sticks.

3. In a bowl, mix egg, milk, maple syrup, vanilla, and cinnamon.

4. Dip the bread-sticks in the egg mixture. Coat well, but shake off the excess.

5. Place the coated sticks in batches on the parchment and spray with olive oil spray.

6. Cover your instant pot with a Mealthy crisp lid and cook for 10 minutes. Flip after 5 minutes. The time needed to cook may vary as per your desired crispiness.

7. Serve with mayo or hot sauce and enjoy.

Nutrition Facts Per Serving

Calories 160 Protein 6.9g Carbohydrates 25.9g Fat 3.2g

Avocado Egg Rolls

Prep Time: 20 minutes, Cook Time: 7 minutes; Serves 10

Ingredients

3 Hass avocados, cubed

1 small lime, juiced

1 Roma tomato, chopped

1/2 cup diced red onion

1/2 cup chopped fresh cilantro

kosher salt to taste

10 egg roll wrappers

1 egg, beaten

cooking spray

Instructions

1. Combine avocado, lime juice, tomato, red onion, cilantro, and salt in a bowl. Gently toss to combine.

2. Fill each egg roll wrapper with an avocado mixture below the center of the wrapper. Now fold the roll from bottom and tuck under. Fold from both sides and then roll it up tightly. Seal the wrapper with beaten egg. Repeat until all egg rolls are complete.

3. Spray CrispLid fryer basket with cooking spray.

4. Put eggs rolls in a row in CrispLid air fryer basket. Spray the rolls with cooking spray. Place the CrispLid trivet inside the steel pot of the cooker and put the basket at top of the trivet.

5. Close the lid and plug it in. Set the temperature to 400°F and cook for 4 minutes; Cook for 3-4 more minutes and keep flipping the rolls until they become light brown. Repeat with remaining egg rolls.

Nutrition Facts Per Serving

Calories 190 Fat 8g Carbohydrates 23.7g Protein 6g

Breakfast Frittata

Prep time: 10 minutes, Cook time: 17 minutes; Serves 6

Ingredients

6 large eggs

6 tablespoons half-and-half

3/4 teaspoon kosher salt

1/4 teaspoon ground black pepper

3 cups spinach

3/4 cup diced onion

1/3 cup diced tomatoes

1/3 cup shredded Cheddar cheese

1/3 cup feta cheese

Cooking spray

1 sliced green onion

Instructions

6. Whisk eggs, half-and-half, salt, and black pepper together in a bowl; Then add onion, spinach, tomato, cheddar cheese, and feta cheese and mix it well.

7. Coat a deep nonstick 6-inch round pan with cooking spray. Pour the mixture of egg into the pan.

8. Now, place pressure cooker trivet into inner steel pot of pressure cooker and set the pan with egg mixture onto the trivet.

9. Place CrispLid on top of the inner steel pot and plugin. Set to 350°F and cook the frittata until set, 17 to 22 minutes. Now, set the lid on the silicone trivet.

10. Top frittata with green onions and it is ready to serve.

Nutrition Facts Per Serving

Calories 153 Proteins 10.2g Carbohydrates 4g Fat 10.7g

Spicy Bacon Breakfast

Prep time: 2 min, Cook time: 8 min; Serve 6

Ingredients

12 Bacon Slices

½ Tbsp allspice seasoning

½ Tbsp crushed red pepper flakes
2 Tbsp of sugar

Instructions

1. Combine all the spice mixture in a bowl

2. Dredge the bacon slices in the mix to coat well

3. Transfer to the air fryer basket and place it on the trivet. Later place the trivet in the pot and cover it with crisp Lid.

4. Set the pot to 350°F for 8 minutes. Flip it halfway and keep cooking until crisp.

Nutrition Facts Per Serving

Calories 411 Fat 27g Carbohydrates 19g Protein 23g

Toasted Cheese Sandwich

Prep Time: 5 min, Cook Time: 7 min; Serves 1

Ingredients

2 bread slices

1 Cheese slice

2 tbsp butter

2 slices tomato

1 Slice ham

1 long toothpick

Instructions

1. Arrange the bread. Make sure they are well buttered on the outside. Place a toothpick through its center.

2. Place it in the fryer basket. Put it in the trivet and cover it with the Mealthy lid.

3. Set it on 350°F and let it cook for 7-10 min.

Nutrition Facts Per Serving

Calories 269 Fat 13g Carbohydrates 26g Protein 12g

Crispy Brussels Sprouts

Prep time: 10 minutes, Cook time: 10 minutes; Serves 6

Ingredients

1 1/2 pounds Brussels sprouts, trimmed and halved

2 tablespoons olive oil

3/4 teaspoon salt

1/8 teaspoon ground black pepper, or more to taste

cooking spray

Instructions

1. Mix Brussels sprouts, oil, salt, and black pepper together in a bowl.

2. Spray CrispLid fryer basket with cooking spray and add Brussels sprouts to the basket, working in batches as needed.

3. Put CrispLid trivet in the inner steel pot of the cooker and put fryer basket on the trivet.

4. Plug it in and close the lid. Set the temperature to 400°F and cook Brussels sprouts until browned and crispy, 10 to 15 minutes. Lift the lid using the handle and set it on the silicone trivet.

5. Transfer crispy Brussels sprouts to a serving platter.

Nutrition Facts Per Serving

Calories 80 Protein 3g Carbohydrates 8.1g Fat 4g

Roasted Tomatoes

Prep time: 10 minutes, Cook time: 18 minutes; Serves 4

Ingredients

4 Roma tomatoes, each cut into 1-inch rounds

1 tablespoon olive oil

1 clove garlic, crushed

1 1/2 teaspoons dried basil

1 1/2 teaspoons dried oregano (or herbs de Provence)

2 tsp salt and 1 tsp ground black pepper

Instructions

1. Place the CrispLid at top of inner steel pot and plug it in.

2. Toss tomatoes, olive oil, garlic, basil, oregano, salt, and black pepper together in a large bowl until tomatoes are evenly coated.

3. Put the CrispLid trivet in the inner steel pot of the cooker and fryer basket on top of the trivet. Cut a round piece of parchment paper. Then place it in the CrispLid fryer basket. Transfer tomatoes to CrispLid fryer basket, arranging in a single layer and working in batches as needed.

4. Set to 350°F. Cook for 15 minutes; flip tomatoes and continue cooking until the desired doneness is reached, 3 to 5 minutes more. Lift the lid using the handle and set it on the silicone mat.

Nutrition Facts Per Serving

Calories 54 Protein 1g Carbohydrates 3.6g Fat 4g

Reuben Egg Rolls

Prep time: 20 minutes, Cook time: 10 minutes; Serves 8

Ingredients

4 ounces cream cheese

2 tablespoons Russian Dressing, plus more for dipping

1 tablespoon prepared horseradish

3/4 pound sliced corned beef, chopped

1 1/2 cups shredded Swiss cheese

1/2 cup sauerkraut, drained

16 egg roll wrappers

1 egg, beaten

cooking spray

Instructions

1. Mix cream cheese, Russian dressing, and horseradish together in a bowl; stir in corned beef, Swiss cheese, and sauerkraut until evenly combined.

2. Fill each egg roll wrapper with a corned beef mixture. Fold the bottom point over the filling and tuck under. Fold both sides and then tightly roll it up. Seal the wrapper with beaten egg. Repeat until all egg rolls are complete.

3. Spray CrispLid fryer basket with cooking spray.

4. Add the egg rolls in a single row in the CrispLid air fryer basket. Use cooking spray to spray over the rolls. Place the CrispLid trivet inside the steel pot of the cooker and fryer basket at the top of the trivet.

5. Close the lid and plug it in. Set the temperature to 400°F and cook for 5 minutes; Flip the side and cook for 5 more minutes. Repeat with remaining egg rolls.

6. Serve egg rolls with Russian dressing on the side for dipping.

Nutrition Facts Per Serving

Calories 437 Protein 21g Carbohydrates 41.1g Fat 21g

Smoky mashed eggplant

Prep time: 20 Min, Cook Time: 23 Min; Serves 4

Ingredients

Roasted Eggplant:

4 eggplant

4 green chile peppers, sliced

4 cloves garlic

cooking spray

Roasted Smashed Eggplants:

2 tablespoons vegetable oil

3 tomatoes, finely chopped

1 tablespoon minced fresh ginger

1 teaspoon cumin seeds

1 large onion, finely chopped

1/2 teaspoon turmeric

1 1/2 teaspoons ground cumin

1 1/2 teaspoons ground coriander

1 teaspoon Kashmiri red chili powder

2 tsp Salt according to taste

Instructions

1. Make 3 slits in each eggplant and stuff the slits with the green chili and garlic cloves. Spray cooking spray overstuffed eggplant and place it in a single layer in the CrispLid fryer basket.

2. Set CrispLid trivet in the inner steel pot of pressure cooker fryer basket on top of the trivet.

3. Set inner steel pot to 400°F (200°C) and cook for 10 minutes. Flip eggplant and continue cooking for about another 10 minutes, until it is browned and completely softened. Lift the lid using the handle.

4. Remove eggplant's skin once it is completely roasted in the fryer basket.

5. Add oil in the cooker and select the sauté option.

6. Stir ginger and cumin seeds into the hot oil. Cook and stir onion for 3 min, until it is light golden brown

7. Mix tomato, red chili powder, turmeric, coriander, cumin, and salt into onion mixture. Now add the peeled eggplant and mash them using a potato masher until softened. Stir water and peas into the mixture. Press Cancel.

8. Serve eggplant dish hot and garnish with cilantro.

Nutrition Facts Per Serving

Calories 397 Protein 10g Carbohydrates 69.4g Fat 9g

Pressure Cooker Scalloped Potatoes

Prep Time: 10 minutes, Cook Time: 8 minutes; Serves 6

Ingredients

6 small gold potatoes, cut into ¼ inch thick slices

170.097g/6lb sharp white, grated Cheddar cheese

42.524g/1 ½lb mild, grated Cheddar cheese

4 ½ tablespoons heavy cream

¾ teaspoon kosher salt

Instructions

1. Put potatoes into the inner steel pot of pressure cooker and add water.

2. Set steam vent to Sealing after placing the lid. Select Pressure Cook (manual) and cook for 1 minute. Set the steam vent to Venting to release pressure.

3. Transfer the potatoes to a round baking dish leaving the water behind.

4. Set pressure cooker to Sauté on High.

5. Mix rest of the ingredients - white Cheddar cheese, heavy cream, garlic powder, salt, and black pepper with the remaining liquid in the pot. Stir until the cheese sauce is smooth. Select Cancel to stop Sauté. Unplug the cooker.

6. Pour the potatoes in the sauce, coat them properly. Sprinkle mild Cheddar cheese over potatoes. Put CrispLid on top of the inner steel pot and set it to 500°F (260°C). Cook till the potatoes turn brown and the cheese is bubbling. Lift the lid and set the potatoes on the silicone trivet. Let it cool, then serve.

Nutrition Facts Per Serving

Calories 316 Protein 12g Carbohydrates 31g Fat 16g

Rosemary Potatoes

Prep Time: 10 minutes, Cook Time: 14 minutes; Serves 6

Ingredients

2 pounds small red or white potatoes, quartered

2 tablespoons olive oil

2 tablespoons minced fresh rosemary leaves

3/4 teaspoon kosher salt

1/2 teaspoon freshly ground black pepper

Instructions

1. Combine potatoes, olive oil, rosemary, salt, and black pepper in a large bowl until potatoes are evenly coated.

2. Arrange potatoes in a single layer in CrispLid fryer basket, working in batches as needed. Place the CrispLid trivet inside the inner steel pot of the cooker and set the fryer basket at the top of the trivet.

3. Place the CrispLid at the top of the inner steel pot and then plug it in. Set the temperature at 425°F and cook for 7 minutes; carefully flip potatoes using tongs. Cook for 7 to 8 minutes more until the potatoes become crispy on the outside and tender from inside.

Nutrition Facts Per Serving

Calories 97.8 Protein 1g Carbohydrates 12.2g Fat 5g

Chapter 3 Snacks

Sweet Potato Fries

Prep time: 10 minutes, Cook time: 16 minutes; Serves 2

Ingredients

1/2 teaspoon salt

1/2 teaspoon garlic powder

1/2 teaspoon chili powder

1/4 teaspoon ground cumin

2 tablespoons olive oil

2 large sweet potatoes, cut into ½-inch thick strips

Instructions

1. Take a large bowl and add salt, garlic powder, chili powder, and cumin and combine them all.

2. Whisk olive oil into salt mixture, and then add sweet potato strips and toss to coat.

3. Now without overlapping, place as many sweet potato strips into the basket of Crisplid fryer basket, and working in batches if needed.

4. Plug-in the wire and set CrispLid on top of the inner steel pot. Set to 425°F and cook for 16 to 20 minutes until desired crispiness is reached. Lift the lid and set it on the silicone mat. Repeat with remaining strips.

Nutrition Facts Per Serving

Calories 298.8 Protein 4g Carbohydrates 39.2g Fat 14g

Nachos

Prep time: 10 min, Cook time: 4 min; Serves 2

Ingredients

cooking spray

1 cup tortilla chips

1/4 cup shredded cooked chicken

1/4 cup pico de gallo

1/4 cup black beans

1/2 cup Mexican cheese blend

Instructions

1. Spray CrispLid fryer basket with cooking spray.

2. Layer half the chips, half the black beans, half the chicken, half the pico de gallo, and half the Mexican cheese blend in the prepared fryer basket. Repeat layering with remaining chips, black beans, chicken, pico de gallo, and Mexican cheese blend.

3. Set the CrispLid to 400°F (200°C) and cook until cheese is bubbling and lightly browned, about 4 minutes.

Nutrition Facts Per Serving

Calories 252 Fat 14g Carbohydrates 17.5g Protein 14g

Home fries

Prep time: 5 min, Cook time: 25 min; Serves 2

Ingredients

2 small Yukon Gold potatoes, scrubbed and chopped into ½-inch cubes

cooking spray

1/8 teaspoon chili powder

1/8 teaspoon garlic powder

1/4 teaspoon kosher salt

freshly ground black pepper

Instructions

1. Place potatoes in a large bowl. Soak it in water for at least 15 minutes. Drain the water and use a paper towel to pat dry.

2. Spray potatoes with cooking spray and season it with salt.

3. Set the Mealthy CrispLid to 400°F (200°C) and cook for 10 minutes. Flip home fries and cook for 10 minutes more.

4. Spray potatoes with cooking spray and sprinkle half the chili powder, black pepper over potatoes and half the garlic powder. Toss the potatoes and cook for another 5 minutes.

Serve it hot with ketchup!

Nutrition Facts Per Serving

Calories 134 Fat 0g Carbohydrates 29.6g Protein 4g

Vegetable and cheese quesadillas

Prep time: 10 min, Cook time: 8 min; Serves 2

Ingredients

2 (6 inch) flour tortillas

1/2 cup shredded Cheddar cheese

1/2 zucchini, sliced

1/2 red bell pepper, sliced

cooking spray

Instructions

1. Spray 1 side of a single tortilla generously with cooking spray and place flat in CrispLid fryer basket.

2. Spread half the Cheddar cheese over tortilla. Cover the top layer with cheese, bell pepper and zucchini. Cover the top with cheddar cheese.

3. Set Mealthy CrispLid to 400°F and cook for 4 minutes. Keep flipping quesadilla using tongs for 4-5 minutes. Cook until cheese is melted and tortillas are crisp.

Nutrition Facts Per Serving

Calories 291 Fat 13g Carbohydrates 31.5g Protein 12g

Honey Soy-Glazed Tofu

Prep time: 10 minutes, Cook time: 15 minutes; Serves 4

Ingredients

1 package(16 ounces) extra-firm tofu

1/4 cup cornstarch

cooking spray

1/4 cup soy sauce

1 tablespoon rice wine vinegar

1 tablespoon sambal oelek (or Sriracha sauce)

1 tablespoon honey

1 tablespoon chopped chives (optional)

Instructions

1. Take a plate with paper towels and place the drained tofu on top of it. Now put the paper towels over the tofu, and put pressure on it using a heavy object like a cookbook. Pressing needs to be done for at least 15 min.

2. Place the CrispLid at the top of the inner steel pot and plug-in. Set to 450°F.

3. Cut tofu into 1-inch cubes and toss in a large bowl with cornstarch. Now transfer tofu to the CrispLid fryer basket in a single layer, working in batches as needed, and spray cooking spray on all sides of the tofu.

4. Put CrispLid trivet in the inner steel pot of the pressure cooker and place the fryer basket at the top of the trivet.

5. Now cook the tofu for 8 minutes. Shake the basket and keep cooking for about 7 more minutes until the tofu is crisp. Lift the lid and set it on the silicone mat. Repeat the same with the remaining tofu.

6. Cook and stir soy sauce, vinegar, sambal oelek, and honey together in a wide skillet or pot over medium heat until sauce is reduced by half, 2 to 3 minutes. Remove from heat.

7. Transfer cooked tofu directly into the sauce in the skillet and stir until coated.

8. Top the tofu with chives.

Nutrition Facts Per Serving

Calories 77 Protein 4g Carbohydrates 13.2g Fat 1g

Butternut Squash

Prep time: 15 minutes, Cook time: 12 minutes; Serves 4

Ingredients

2 cups peeled and cubed Butternut squash

1 tablespoon olive oil

1/4 teaspoon salt

1/8 teaspoon ground black pepper

1/8 teaspoon dried thyme

1 tablespoon chopped fresh parsley

Instructions

1. Take a large bowl and mix squash with olive oil, salt, and black pepper thoroughly.

2. Transfer squash to CrispLid fryer basket. Place the CrispLid trivet in the inner steel pot of pressure cooker. Then set the fryer basket above the trivet.

3. Place the CrispLid at the top of the inner steel pot. Set the temperature to 425°F and cook for 6 minutes. Stir butternut squash and continue cooking until browned and tender, about 6 minutes more. Set it on the silicone mat when done.

4. Butternut squash can be garnished with parsley.

Nutrition Facts Per Serving

Calories 68 Protein 0.7g Carbohydrates 8.3g Fat 3.6g

Apple Chips

Prep time: 10 minutes, Cook time: 8 minutes; Serves 2

Ingredients

1 Packet of Apple Chips

1 tablespoon white sugar

1/2 teaspoon ground cinnamon

1 apple, cut into ⅛-inch thick pieces using a mandolin

Coconut Cream Dip

1/2 cup chilled coconut cream

1 tablespoon maple syrup, or more to taste

2 teaspoons lemon juice

1 teaspoon vanilla extract

Instructions

1. Take a bowl and make a mixture of sugar and cinnamon.

2. Dip apple slices into cinnamon and sugar mixture, coating evenly on 1 side only.

3. Arrange coated apple slices in the CrispLid fryer basket in a single layer, working in batches. Set the trivet in the inner steel pot of the cooker and set the fryer basket at top of the trivet.

4. Close the lid and plug it in the socket. Set the temperature to 375°F and cook for 4 minutes. Flip the side and cook for 4 to 6 minutes.

5. Beat coconut cream in a bowl using an electric mixer on medium speed until fluffy, about 4 minutes. Make the addition of maple syrup, lemon juice, and vanilla extract; stir until coconut cream dip is well-mixed.

6. Transfer apple chips to a bowl and let cool; serve with coconut cream dip.

Nutrition Facts Per Serving

Calories 375 Protein 1g Carbohydrates 65.8g Fat 12g

Cheesy Garlic Bread

Prep time: 10 minutes, Cook time: 5 minutes; Serves 6

Ingredients

1 French baguette

1/4 cup butter, softened

2 teaspoons of garlic powder

2 tsp fine salt and freshly ground black pepper to taste

3/4 cup shredded Cheddar cheese

1/4 cup shredded mozzarella cheese

100g chopped fresh parsley

Instructions

1. Take the baguette and then slice it into thirds, and then cut each third lengthwise, into long rectangles.

2. Spread softened butter on the inside of bread slices. Now sprinkle the garlic powder, salt, and black pepper over butter.

3. Sprinkle Cheddar cheese and mozzarella cheese over butter and seasoning mixture on each bread slice.

4. Place slices into CrispLid fryer basket and place the cheese side up. Set the CrispLid trivet in the inner steel pot of the cooker and set the fryer basket on top of the trivet.

5. Close the lid and plug-in. Set to 425°F and cook until the cheese has melted about 5 minutes. Lift the lid using the handle and set it on the silicone mat.

6. Garnish each cheesy garlic bread with parsley.

Nutrition Facts Per Serving

Calories 284 Protein 10g Carbohydrates 29.6g Fat 14g

Fried Pickles

Prep time: 10 minutes, Cook time: 8 minutes; Serves 4

Ingredients

1/2 cup buttermilk

1 (16 ounces) jar dill pickle chips

1 1/4 cups cornmeal

1/2 cup all-purpose flour

1 teaspoon garlic powder

cooking spray

Instructions

1. Stir buttermilk in a shallow bowl; add pickles and stir to coat.

2. Stir cornmeal, flour, and garlic powder in a separate shallow bowl.

3. Remove pickles from the buttermilk. Add pickles to cornmeal mixture; toss until coated evenly.

4. Place the pickles in one layer in the CrispLid fryer basket and use cooking spray to coat the pickles.

5. Place the CrispLid trivet inside the steel pot of pressure cooker and place the fryer basket at the top of the trivet.

6. Close the lid and plug it in. Set the temperature to 400°F and cook for 4 minutes. Flip pickles using tongs and cook for 4 more minutes until the coating is crispy.

Nutrition Facts Per Serving

Calories 239 Protein 6g Carbohydrates 49.3g Fat 2g

Corn on the Cob

Prep time: 2 minutes, Cook time: 10 minutes; Serves 3

Ingredients

3 corn on the cob (husks removed)

Cooking oil spray/butter

50g Freshly chopped cilantro/coriander

2 tsp Salt

1/2 tsp Pepper

2 tablespoon lemon zest

Instructions

1. Place the corn in a bowl and spray some olive oil over it. You may use butter as well.

2. Add salt and pepper to taste.

3. Place the corn into your instant pot and cover it with a Mealthy Crisp Lid.

4. Cook for 10 minutes, turning the corn a couple of times during cooking so that it cooks evenly.

5. Serve with some extra salt, lemon zest, and freshly chopped cilantro.

Nutrition Facts Per Serving

Calories 9 Protein 0.5g Carbohydrates 1.6g Fat 0.1g

Chicken Nuggets

Prep time: 5 minutes, Cook time: 10 minutes; Serves 6

Ingredients

Nuggets:

olive oil cooking spray

1 lb boneless chicken tenders, cut into 40 bite-sized pieces

2 cups brown rice cereal

½ tsp cayenne

½ tsp paprika

1 tsp garlic powder

½ tsp Salt

1 egg white

2 tablespoons hot sauce

2 tsp olive oil

Dipping Sauce:-

¾ cup plain Greek Yogurt

2 tablespoon hot sauce

⅓ cup blue cheese crumbles

1 tablespoon white wine vinegar

1 tablespoon lemon juice

Instructions

1. Put the rice cereal in a bag along with the spices.

2. Use a rolling pin to crush cereal, leaving some larger pieces intact. Put the cereal mixture in a bowl.

3. Whisk egg white, hot sauce, and olive oil in another bowl.

4. Dip the chicken bites one by one into the hot sauce mixture and then into the cereal spice mixture. Shake off the excess.

5. Place the nuggets in your instant pot in small batches and spray with olive oil.

6. Cover the pot with a Mealthy crisp lid and cook for 4 minutes. Post this, flip the nuggets and spray with olive oil. Cook for an additional 4 minutes.

7. For the hot sauce, mix the Greek yogurt, hot sauce vinegar, lemon, and blue cheese crumbles together.

8. Serve the nuggets with sauce and enjoy it.

Nutrition Facts Per Serving

Calories 384 Protein 31.1g Carbohydrates 50.4 Fat 6.5g

Chickpea Crisp

Prep time: 10 Min, Cook Time: 16 Min; Serves 4

Ingredients

1 (15 ounces) can chickpeas, rinsed and patted dry with paper towels

1/2 teaspoon dried rosemary

1 tablespoon olive oil

1/4 teaspoon mustard powder

1/2 teaspoon dried thyme

1/4 teaspoon salt

Instructions

1. Twitch the chickpeas, dried thyme, olive oil, mustard powder, dried rosemary, and salt together in a large bowl.

2. Spread chickpeas in a single layer in the CrispLid fryer basket. Do the working in batches as required. Set the CrispLid trivet in inner steel pot of pressure cooker and on the top of it set the fryer basket on top of the trivet.

3. Set Mealthy CrispLid temperature to 400°F (200 °C) and let the chickpeas sit for 8 minutes and then shake the basket. Continue cooking it for another 8 minutes and then check chickpeas again. Continue cooking in 2-minute increments until it reaches the desired crispness.

Nutrition Facts Per Serving

Calories 67 Protein 2g Carbohydrates 5.8g Fat 4g

Black Eyed Peas

Prep time: 3 min, Cook time: 50 min; Serves 6

Ingredients

1 pound dried black-eyed peas

6.5 cups water (might vary a little)

2 Tbsp chicken flavor (you can also choose beef or vegetable)

½ cup crumbled bacon

Instructions

1. Add the ingredients to the Mealthy Lid pot

2. Make sure that the knob is turned to sealing

3.Set the pressure to high for 30 min.

4. If you like it extra soft, then cook it for 20-25 min instead of 30 min.

Nutrition Facts Per Serving

Calories 205 Protein 13g Carbohydrates 36g Fat 1g

Roasted Chickpea

Prep time: 10 Min, Cook Time: 15 Min; Serves 4

Ingredients

20 ounces chickpeas, rinsed and patted dry with paper towels

1/2 teaspoon dried rosemary

1/2 teaspoon dried thyme

1/2 teaspoon salt

1 tablespoon olive oil

1 tablespoon cornflour

Instructions

1. Mix chickpeas, cornfloor, dried thyme, olive oil, dried rosemary, and salt in a large bowl.

2. Place chickpeas in the CrispLid fryer basket.

3. Set Mealthy CrispLid temperature to 400°F and cook for 8 minutes. Shake after every 2 minutes.

4. Continue cooking for another 7 minutes or until crisp.

5. Serve hot with mint mayo.

Nutrition Facts Per Serving

Calories 77 Protein 2g Carbohydrates 6g Fat 5g

Masala Peanuts

Prep Time: 5 minutes, Cook Time: 15 minutes; Serves 4

Ingredients

1 cup red Spanish peanuts/Unsalted roasted peanuts

5 tablespoon chickpea flour

1/2 teaspoon cayenne pepper

1/2 teaspoon cumin seeds

Cooking spray

Instructions

1. Mix water, chickpea flour, oil, turmeric, cayenne, cumin, and salt together in a bowl until it turns into a batter form. Add peanuts and mix well.

2. Set the fryer basket on top of the trivet after setting it in the inner steel pot of the pressure cooker. Add the mixture to the basket and spray cooking spray onto it.

3. Place the CrispLid at the top of the inner steel pot and then plug it in. Set the temperature at 325°F and cook for 10 minutes.

4. Remove the lid and break up any peanuts that may have stuck together. Spray the cooking spray again.

5. Place the CrispLid at top of the inner steel pot. Set the temperature at 400°F and cook until the outsides for about 5 minutes more.

6. Remove peanuts from the fryer basket and let it cool before serving.

Nutrition Facts Per Serving

Calories 467 Proteins 15g Carbohydrates 23.1g Fat 35g

Old Bay Chicken Wings

Prep time: 10 minutes; Cook time: 15 minutes; Serves 4

Ingredients

Cooking spray

1 pound chicken wings

1/4 cup unsalted butter, melted

1 1/2 teaspoons seafood seasoning (such as Old Bay(R)), plus more for dusting

1/2 lemon, juiced

Instructions

1. Spray CrispLid basket with cooking spray. Lay chicken wings in a single layer in the basket, working in batches as needed.

2. Place trivet in inner steel pot of the cooker. Place fryer basket on the trivet. Set CrispLid on top of inner steel pot and plug in.

3. Set CrispLid temperature at 425°F. Cook chicken wings until a thermometer inserted near the bone reads at least 165°F, 15 to 20 minutes.

4. Melt butter in a small skillet over medium heat; whisk in Old Bay seasoning and lemon juice.

5. Transfer wings to a bowl and pour butter mixture on top and toss to coat. Dust wings with additional Old Bay seasoning as desired.

Nutrition Facts Per Serving

Calories 312 Protein 32.9g Carbohydrates 0.1g Fat 20.1g

Onion Rings

Prep Time: 20 minutes, Cook Time: 10 minute; Serves 4

Ingredients

1 cup all-purpose flour, divided

1/2 teaspoon fine sea salt

1/2 cup buttermilk

1 egg

1 cup plain bread crumbs

1 large sweet yellow onion, cut into ½-inch thick rings and separated

cooking spray

Instructions

1. Combine ¾ cup flour and salt in a shallow dish. Beat remaining flour, buttermilk, and egg together in a separate shallow dish until smooth and thickened. Add the bread crumbs to a shallow dish.

2. Lightly dredge onion rings in flour. Dip onions ring into the buttermilk mixture and drain excess liquid. Dredge onion rings in bread crumbs until evenly coated.

3. Spray CrispLid fryer basket and onion rings with cooking spray and arrange onion rings in a single layer in the fryer basket, working in batches as needed.

4. Place CrispLid trivet in the inner steel pot of pressure cooker and put fryer basket at top of the trivet.

5. Close the lid and place it at the top of the inner steel pot. Plug it in. Set the temperature to 400°F and cook onion rings for 5 minutes. Flip onion rings till they become brown and crispy, it may take 5-7 minutes more. Repeat the same steps with remaining onion rings.

Nutrition Facts Per Serving

Calories 268 Protein 10g Carbohydrates 48.1g Fat 4g

Chapter 4 Poultry and Meat

Chicken Taquitos

Prep time: 5 minutes, Cook time: 30 minutes; Serves 2

Ingredients

1 lb chicken tenderloins

1 jar of organic salsa

1 lime

2 tsp salt

1 cup of shredded cheddar

8 corn tortillas/ gluten-free whole wheat flour tortillas

Olive oil/ avocado oil cooking spray

1 tsp salt-free taco seasoning

A small pack of Greek yogurt (optional)

Instructions

1. Place the chicken in your instant pot and top it with salsa.
2. Lock the lit and press the manual/pressure cook button. Let it set for 15 minutes.
3. Once cooked, allow a natural release.
4. Shred the chicken and squeeze some fresh lime juice on it.
5. Add 1 tsp salt-free taco seasoning and a pinch of salt.
6. Wrap 4 tortillas at a time in a damp paper towel and microwave for 30 seconds.
7. Place 2 tablespoons of shred chicken on the top edge of the tortilla and add 1.5 tablespoons of cheddar.
8. Gently roll the tortillas making a taquito shape and use a toothpick to hold them together.
9. Spray the basket of your instant pot with olive oil and place the tortilla shells in batches of 2-4 at a time.
10. Spray the shells with olive oil and sprinkle some salt over them.
11. Cover the pot with a Mealthy Crisp Lid and set on 390 for a few minutes or until the tortillas are crisp.
12. Do the same for the remaining tortillas.
13. Garnish with avocado or cheese or drizzle some Greek yogurt.

Nutrition Facts Per Serving

Calories 855 Protein 83.2g Carbohydrates 90.9 Fat 17.7g

Lemon Pepper Chicken Wings

Prep time: 5 minutes, Cook time: 22 minutes; Serves 8

Ingredients

2 lb chicken wings

1 tablespoon baking powder

1 teaspoon salt

Cooking spray

1 tablespoon lemon pepper seasoning, divided

1/4 cup butter

1 lemon, sliced

Instructions

1. Toss chicken with baking powder in a bowl until evenly coated and season it with salt.

2. Spray CrispLid basket with cooking spray. Lay chicken in a single layer, skin-side up, in CrispLid fryer basket.

3. Keep the trivet in the inner steel pot of the cooker. Place fryer basket with chicken on the trivet. Then sprinkle 1 teaspoon lemon pepper seasoning over wings.

4. Place CrispLid on top of the inner steel pot and plug-in.

5. Set CrispLid to 425°F. Cook chicken wings for 10 minutes. Change the sides of the wings and cook for another 10 minutes till the temperature reads 165°F. Lift the lid and set it on the silicone mat.

6. Now combine butter and remaining lemon pepper seasoning together in a small skillet over low-medium heat. Cook for 2-3 minutes and stir until butter is melted. Transfer wings to a bowl and drizzle butter mixture over wings. Garnish with sliced lemons.

Nutrition Facts Per Serving

Calories 266 Protein 33g Carbohydrates 1.4g Fat 14.3g

BBQ Chicken Wings

Prep time: 5 minutes, Cook time: 15 minutes; Serves 4

Ingredients

1 pound chicken wings

2 tsp salt to taste

cooking spray

1/3 cup barbeque sauce

Instructions

1. Season chicken with salt.

2. Spray CrispLid fryer basket with cooking spray. Add the chicken in the fryer basket.

3. Put the trivet inside the steel pot of pressure cooker. Place the fryer basket on the trivet. Plug-in the inner steel pot and place the crisp lid on its top.

4. Set CrispLid to 425°F. Cook the chicken wings for about 15-20 minutes until the thermometer reads 165°F.

5. Put the cooked wings to a large bowl, add the sauce and the meal is ready to serve.

Nutrition Facts Per Serving

Calories 411 Protein 19g Carbohydrates 20.8 Fat 28g

Chicken Tenders

Prep time: 15 minutes, Cook time: 10 minutes; Serves 6

Ingredients

1 1/2 pounds boneless chicken breasts, cut into ½-inch thick strips

1 tsp salt and ground black pepper

1 egg

1 cup Italian-style bread crumbs

Cooking spray

Instructions

1. Add salt and black pepper to the chicken.

2. Crack the egg in a shallow dish. Season egg with salt and black pepper and whisk to combine.

3. Add bread crumbs into a separate shallow dish.

4. Dredge chicken tenders through egg wash, then through bread crumbs.

5. Roll chicken in the bread crumbs and press firmly to make the bread crumbs stick.

6. Apply the cooking spray on both sides of chicken tenders and add to the CrispLid fryer basket.

7. Place the CrispLid at the top of the inner steel pot and plug it in. Fix the temperature at 425°F and cook for 5 minutes. Flip chicken tenders and cook for 5 to 7 minutes more until chicken loses its pink color in the center and the outside becomes crispy.

Nutrition Facts Per Serving

Calories 292 Protein 36.4g Carbohydrates 13.5g Fat 10.3g

Spaghetti Squash taco boats

Prep time: 15 minutes, Cook time: 15 minutes; Serves 4

Ingredients

1 lb chicken thighs

1 spaghetti squash (cut in half)

½ chopped onion

2 cloves of minced garlic

½ cup chopped beans

½ tsp pepper

1 tsp chili powder

1 tsp cumin

1 tsp paprika

1 tsp olive oil

½ cup of water

Toppings:

½ cup diced tomatoes

¼ chopped cilantro

1 sliced jalapeno sliced

⅔ cup shredded cheddar

Instructions

1. Set the instant pot to sauté and add olive oil.

2. Sauté the chicken thighs with onions, garlic, and seasoning for 2-3 minutes.

3. Add beans and water to the instant pot and place the trivet over them.

4. Place the spaghetti on the trivet. This will ensure that the squash and chicken separated while cooking.

5. Lock the pot with Mealthy crisp lid and cook for 8 minutes.

6. Once cooked, remove the spaghetti squash first and set it aside.

7. Shred the chicken into chunks using tongs or a fork.

8. It's time to assemble the taco boats. Place the chicken and beans in the center of the spaghetti squash.

9. Top with tomatoes, jalapenos, cilantro, and cheese. Broil for 3-5 minutes to melt and toast the cheese and enjoy.

Nutrition Facts Per Serving

Calories 286 Protein 38.8g Carbohydrates 7.1g Fat 11.4g

Bacon Wrapped Chicken Tenders

Prep time: 5 minutes, Cook time: 20 minutes; Serves 4

Ingredients

1 lb chicken tenderloins

1 package of turkey bacon

20g Sliced pepper jack/sharp cheddar/cheese of your choice

1 avocado

Olive oil spray

10 mg Garlic powder

2 tsp Salt

Instructions

1. Sprinkle ½ tsp of garlic powder and salt on the chicken and wrap each tenderloin with 2 pieces of bacon. Smaller tenderloins may be wrapped with one 1 bacon. You may use a toothpick to keep the bacon secure.

2. Place the bacon-wrapped chicken in your instant pot and spray some olive oil.

3. Cover with Mealthy crisp lid and cook for 10 minutes. Flip the chicken and cook for 8 more minutes. Turn the crisp lid covered pot off.

4. Place half slice of cheese on the bacon-wrapped chicken and leave it in the turned off pot until it melts.

5. Top with 2 tablespoons of sliced avocado and enjoy.

Nutrition Facts Per Serving

Calories 262 Protein 26.7g Carbohydrates 9.7g Fat 13g

Shepherd's Pie

Prep time: 15 minutes, Cook time: 20 minutes; Serves 4

Ingredients

1 lb lean ground turkey	1 tsp salt
olive oil/coconut oil	3 tablespoon tomato paste
1 cup diced carrots	2 cups chopped cauliflower
1 cup diced celery	2 cups peeled and chopped red potatoes
½ chopped onion	2 tablespoon butter/olive oil
1 ½ cup chicken broth	

Instructions

1. Set your instant pot to sauté and spray olive oil.

2. Add in ground turkey cook until brown.

3. Add in the chopped veggies and mix well. Cook for an additional 2 minutes.

4. Remove the turkey and veggies from the pot and place them in a heat-safe dish.

5. Stir in ⅓ cup of chicken broth and tomato paste in the pot and sprinkle ½ tsp of salt. Cover with tin foil.

6. Add cauliflower, potatoes, and a cup of chicken broth to the bottom of your instant pot.

7. Place the trivet on top of the potato and cauliflower mixture and place the dish containing the turkey on top of the trivet.

8. Cover and lock with a Mealthy crisp lid and cook for 7 minutes.

9. After a quick release, drain the potato mixture and reserve the broth.

10. Mash the potatoes right in the pot and add in ½ tsp salt and 2 tablespoons of olive oil/butter. If necessary, add a tablespoon broth as well.

11. Top turkey mixture with mashed potatoes and broil until golden brown.

Nutrition Facts Per Serving

Calories 405 Protein 21g Carbohydrates 39.3 Fat 18.3g

Lasagna

Prep time: 10 minutes; Cook time: 25 minutes; Serves 4

Ingredients

1 lb ground turkey

1 cup cottage cheese/ricotta

1 cup Italian cheese

28 ounces crushed tomatoes

1 tbsp oregano

3 cups of spinach

1 tbsp thyme

1 tbsp parsley

1 tsp black pepper

1 tbsp onion powder

1 tbsp garlic salt

6 whole wheat uncooked lasagna noodles

Instructions

1. Mix Italian cheese and cottage cheese in a bowl.

2. In a separate bowl, mix crushed tomatoes, thyme, parsley, pepper, onion powder, and garlic salt.

3. Add sauce and ½ cup of water to the bottom of your instant pot.

4. Layer the noodles, cheese mix, sauce, uncooked ground turkey, and spinach. Repeat until ¾th of the pot is full.

5. Top with shredded cheese and cover with tin foil.

6. Add 3 cups of water to the bottom of the instant pot and insert the lasagna on the trivet

7. Lock the pot with Mealthy crisp lid and cook for 20 minutes.

8. Allow a natural release.

9. Remove the lasagna from the pot and remove the foil covering as well. Garnish fresh basil.

Nutrition Facts Per Serving

Calories 794 Carbohydrates 62.8g Protein 52.7g Fat 36.9g

Spice-Rubbed Whole Chicken

Prep time: 10 minutes, Cook time: 1 hour; Serves 6

Ingredients

1 whole chicken (preferably 4-5 lbs for a 6-quart instant pot)

1 onion

2 lemons

2 tsp paprika

1 tsp cayenne pepper

1 tsp onion powder

1 tsp thyme

½ tsp garlic powder

1 tsp salt

1 cup chicken broth

2 tablespoon olive oil

Instructions

1. Put quartered onions in an instant pot and pour a cup of chicken broth on them.

2. Pat the chicken with paper towels until it's completely dry.

3. Mix all the spices together in 2 tsp of olive oil and coat the chicken skin with it.

4. Stuff the chicken's cavity with onions, lemon, and fresh thyme

5. Put the sling or trivet on the bottom of the instant pot and place the spice-coated chicken on the top.

6. Cover the pot with a Mealthy Crisp lid and let the chicken cook for at least 30 minutes. In case you use frozen chicken, cook for double the time.

7. You may throw in some seasonal veggies to make the recipe healthier. To enhance the steaming, cover the top of the chicken with tin foil.

Nutrition Facts Per Serving

Calories 160 Protein 27g Carbohydrate 3g Fat 4.5g

Garlic Parmesan Chicken Wings

Prep Time: 5 minutes, Cook Time: 22 minutes; Serves 8

Ingredients

907.1842g/2lb chicken wings

1 tbsp baking powder

Cooking spray

¼ cup butter

1 tbsp chopped fresh parsley

Instructions

1. Add baking powder to a bowl of chicken. Toss it until it is evenly covered with baking powder.

2. Spray the fryer basket with cooking spray. Place the chicken wings in single layers inside the basket in batches.

3. Place CrispLid trivet in the inner pot of pressure cooker. Place basket with chicken at top of the trivet.

4. Place the CrispLid at the top of the inner steel pot and then plug it in.

5. Set CrispLid to 425°F and cook the wings from the skin side. After 10 minutes flip them and cook from the other side for another 10 minutes. Lift the lid using the handle and place it on the silicone mat.

6. Add garlic in butter over medium-low heat until the butter melts.

7. Transfer the wings to a bowl. Add the butter-garlic mixture and parmesan cheese until it is coated evenly.

8. Garnish the final product with Parmesan cheese and parsley.

Nutrition Facts Per Serving

Calories 349 Proteins 11g Carbohydrates 56g Fat 9g

Honey Mustard Chicken Breasts

Prep Time: 10 minutes, Cook Time: 20 minutes; Serves 6

Ingredients

6 boneless, skinless chicken breasts

Cooking spray

6 tablespoons Dijon mustard

3 tablespoons honey

2 tablespoons minced fresh rosemary

Instructions

1. Mix Dijon mustard, honey, rosemary, salt, and black pepper in a bowl.

2. Rub the mixture over the chicken.

3. Spray CrispLid fryer basket with cooking spray. Place coated chicken breasts in the fryer basket.

4. Place the trivet into the steel pot and plugin. Set to 350°F and cook the chicken for 20 to 24 minutes.

5. Place the cooked chicken on the silicone trivet once ready.

Nutrition Facts Per Serving

Calories 236 Proteins 38g Carbohydrates 9.8g Fat 5g

Masala Fried Chicken

Prep Time: 20 minutes, Cook Time: 8 minutes; Serves 6

Ingredients

1 1/2 pounds boneless, skinless chicken thighs

1/2 cup buttermilk

1/4 cup fresh cilantro leaves

2 serrano chile peppers, stemmed

1/2 inch piece fresh ginger, peeled

2 cloves garlic

8 curry leaves (optional)

1 teaspoon salt, or to taste

Coating to be done

3/4 cup rolled oats

1 tablespoon whole black peppercorns

1/4 cup rice flour

1/4 cup all-purpose flour

1 teaspoon salt, or to taste

1 tablespoon coconut oil, or as needed

Instructions

1. Cut each chicken thigh in half, trim extra Fat, and pound to flatten the pieces; transfer to a bowl.

2. Combine buttermilk, cilantro, serrano chile peppers, ginger, garlic, curry leaves, and 1 teaspoon of salt in a blender or food processor and blend until marinade is evenly combined. There will be some texture to the marinade.

3. Pour marinade over chicken; cover and marinate in the refrigerator, 3 hours to overnight.

4. Add rolled oats and peppercorns to blender or food processor and process until oats are fine; mix in rice flour, all-purpose flour, and 1 teaspoon of salt. Transfer oat mixture to a shallow bowl.

5. Remove chicken from marinade and discard marinade. Dredge chicken in oat mixture until well coated and dry to touch. Shake any excess oat mixture back into the bowl.

6. Place the CrispLid trivet inside the inner steel pot of pressure cooker. Also, set the fryer basket at the top of the trivet. Place coated chicken pieces in one layer in the fryer basket, working in batches. Drizzle coconut oil over chicken.

7. Put the CrispLid at the top of the inner steel pot and plug it in the socket. Set the temperature to 450°F and cook until no longer pink in the center, about 8 minutes. A thermometer should read the temperature of at least 165°F.

8. Repeat a similar procedure with the left chicken.

Nutrition Facts Per Serving

Calories 306 Protein 31g Carbohydrates 18.5g Fat 12g

Korean Chicken Wings

Prep Time: 10 minutes, Cook Time: 16 minutes; Serves 6

Ingredients

Chicken:

1 pound chicken wings and drumettes

1 1/2 teaspoons baking powder

1 pinch salt

cooking spray

Glaze:

1 tablespoon soy sauce

1 tablespoon yuzu jam

1 1/2 teaspoons raw cane sugar

1 1/2 teaspoons water

1 clove garlic, thinly sliced

1/2 teaspoon thinly sliced fresh ginger, or to taste

Toppings:

1 green onion, thinly sliced

1 tablespoon chopped, toasted walnuts

Instructions

1. Toss chicken with baking powder in a bowl; season with salt.

2. Spray CrispLid basket with cooking spray. Put the chicken in a single row in the basket.

3. Place the trivet inside the inner steel pot of the pressure cooker. Place the basket with chicken over the trivet.

4. Place the CrispLid at the top of the inner steel pot and then plug it in.

5. Set CrispLid to 425°F. Cook chicken wings until a thermometer inserted near the bone read at least 165°F, 15 to 20 minutes.

6. Whisk soy sauce, yuzu jam, sugar, water, garlic, and ginger together in a small skillet over medium heat. Bring it to a boiling temperature; Then reduce the heat and simmer until soy-yuzu glaze is reduced by half, 1 to 2 minutes.

7. Transfer wings to a bowl and drizzle soy-yuzu glaze over wings. Garnish wings with green onion and walnuts.

Nutrition Facts Per Serving

Calories 456 Protein 22g Carbohydrates 17.8g Fat 33g

Chapter 5 Fish and Seafood

Asian Salmon

Prep time: 10 minutes, Cook time: 10 minutes; Serves 4

Ingredients

2 tablespoons soy sauce

1 tablespoon brown sugar

2 teaspoons cornstarch

1 teaspoon Sriracha hot sauce

cooking spray

4 (6 ounces) salmon fillets

Instructions

1. Whisk soy sauce, brown sugar, cornstarch, and Sriracha together in a bowl until smooth.

2. Rinse and dry the salmon fillets. Spray CrispLid fryer basket with cooking spray.

3. Place salmon fillets skin-side down in CrispLid fryer basket. Brush fillets generously with soy sauce mixture using a pastry brush.

4. Place the CrispLid trivet inside the steel pot of the cooker and put the fryer basket at the top of the trivet.

5. Plug-in the inner steel pot and put CrispLid at the top of it. Set the temperature at 375°F and cook for 5 minutes. Brush salmon with more soy sauce mixture and continue cooking until fish flakes easily with a fork, 5 to 7 minutes.

Nutrition Facts Per Serving

Calories 474 Protein 51g Carbohydrates 4.7g Fat 28g

Coconut Shrimp with sweet chili sauce

Prep time: 5 minutes, Cook time: 6 minutes; Serves 4

Ingredients

1 lb large shrimp (18-20 pieces)

½ cup whole wheat breadcrumbs

½ cup unsweetened and shredded coconut

4 tsp raw sugar

Salt to taste

2 tablespoons gluten-free flour/whole wheat flour

1 whole egg

1 egg white
1 tsp arrowroot/cornstarch

cooking oil spray

Sweet Chili Dipping Sauce:

2 cloves of minced garlic

1 tablespoon grated ginger

5 tablespoons white vinegar

3 tablespoons maple syrup/honey

2 tablespoons Coconut Aminos

½ tsp chili paste

Instructions

1. For the sauce, place all the sauce ingredients in a small saucepan and cook over medium heat for 2-3 minutes or until the sauce bubbles.

2. Once the sauce thickens, set aside and allow it to cool.

3. Mix coconut flakes, breadcrumbs, sugar, and salt in a bowl.

4. Place the flour in another small bowl.

5. Whisk a whole egg in another bowl.

6. Dip the shrimp in the flour, then into the egg bowl, and then in the coconut crumb mixture. Shake off the excess.

7. Spray your instant pot with cooking spray place the shrimp over it.

8. Spray oil on the shrimp as well and cover the pot with a Mealthy crisp lid.

9. Cook the shrimp, in batches for at least 4 minutes on one side. Post this, flip and cook 2 more minutes.

10. Serve with the dipping sauce and enjoy.

Nutrition Facts Per Serving

Calories 214 Protein 24.4g Carbohydrates 25.5g Fat 1.7g

Instant Pot Shrimp

Prep time: 10 Min, Cook Time: 1 Min; Serves 4

Ingredients

28 oz frozen shrimp (deveined and peeled if possible)

½ cup apple cider vinegar

½ cup water

Creole seasoning to taste

Instruction

1. Put everything into instant pot

2. Close the lid and seal the top valve

3. Program for Manual high for 1 minute

4. Quickly release the lid when the timer goes off

5. Serve it hot!

Nutrition Facts Per Serving

Calories 73 Protein 15g Carbohydrates 1g Fat 1g

Salmon cake

Prep time: 5 min, Cook time: 15 min; Serves 2

Ingredients

7 ounces salmon-cooked leftover

12 Ritz or club (stacked sized) crackers

1 egg

⅓ cup panko seasoned with salt & pepper

Instructions

1. Crack and whisk the egg into a medium bowl using a fork.

2. Add the leftover salmon into flakes to the bowl, using your hands.

3. Make a mixture so that you can make a ball using your palm.

4. Roll the ball into this loose flaky mixture to cover all the edges.

5. Once it starts looking like a panko-coated hockey puck, spray it lightly with cooking oil and set it on the greased baking rack.

6. Keep changing the sides and make sure both sides are well sprayed with cooking oil.

7. Flip them gently and place them inside the oven or pan with Mealthy lid for 7 minutes.

Nutrition Facts Per Serving

Calories 181 Protein 13g Carbohydrates 3g Fat 13g

Salmon Tikka

Prep Time: 10 minutes, Cook Time: 8 minutes; Serves 6

Ingredients

1/2 lb Skinless salmon

1lb Marinade

2 tablespoons olive oil

1 teaspoon garam masala

½ teaspoon smoked paprika

Instructions

1. Prepare a marinade by combining 2 tablespoon olive oil, garlic, lemon juice, red chili powder, ginger, salt, and smoked paprika. Whisk it until smooth. Add salmon to the marinade and stir properly.

2. Place CrispLid trivet in the inner pot of pressure cooker.

3. Coat the CrispLid fryer basket with ½ teaspoon of olive oil before placing it over the trivet.

4. Place marinated salmon on the fryer basket in a single layer, in batches.

5. Put CrispLid on top of the inner pot and set it to 400°F after plugging in.

6. Cook salmon until it separates with a fork, about 8 minutes.

7. Lift the lid and set it on the silicon trivet.

8. After cooking the other batches, transfer them to a plate and enjoy!

Nutrition Facts Per Serving

Calories 315 Proteins 26g Carbohydrates 3.4g Fat 22g

Tandoori Fish Tikka

Prep Time: 20 minutes, Cook Time: 15 minutes; Serves 8

Ingredients

2lb Marinade

1/4 cup Greek-style yogurt

2 tablespoons canola oil

1 tablespoon ginger-garlic paste (or ½-inch piece ginger and 4 cloves garlic)

1 tablespoon lemon juice

2 teaspoons dried coriander

2 teaspoons dried fenugreek

1 1/2 teaspoons garam masala

1 teaspoon ground cumin

1 teaspoon Kashmiri red chili powder

1 teaspoon salt

1/2 teaspoon turmeric

Tikka Ingredients

1 pound white fish (such as sole), cut into 1½-inch pieces

1 red bell pepper, cut into 1-inch pieces

1 onion, cut into 1-inch pieces and separated

Instructions

1. Mix yogurt, canola oil, garlic-ginger paste, lemon juice, coriander powder, fenugreek, garam masala, cumin, red chili powder, salt, and turmeric together in a bowl until marinade is smooth. Add fish, bell pepper, and onion and stir until evenly coated.

2. Place the CrispLid trivet inside the inner steel pot of the cooker and put the fryer basket at top of the trivet. Arrange marinated fish, bell pepper, and onion in a single layer onto the fryer basket, working in batches as needed.

3. At the top of the inner steel pot, set the CrispLid and then plug it in. Set the temperature at 400°F and cook until fish flakes easily with a fork, about 8 minutes.

Nutrition Facts Per Serving

Calories 324.4 Protein 30g Carbohydrates 10.6g Fat 18g

Mango Shrimps Tacos

Prep Time: 15 minutes, Cook Time: 9 minutes; Serves 4

Ingredients

Shrimp

1 pound shrimp, peeled and deveined

1 tablespoon Cholula hot sauce

1 tablespoon olive oil

2 tsp salt and freshly ground black pepper

50 gm Tortillas

cooking spray

8 corn tortillas

Lime Crema

1/3 cup sour cream

1 lime, juiced

3 tsp salt to taste

Toppings

1/2 cup thinly sliced mango

1 avocado, thinly sliced

1/4 red onion, thinly sliced

1/4 cup chopped fresh cilantro

Instructions

1. Place shrimp, Cholula, and olive oil in a large bowl and toss to evenly coat the shrimp. Add salt and pepper to it and then toss it again. Marinate at room temperature for 10 minutes or in the refrigerator for up to 2 hours.

2. Spray CrispLid fryer basket with cooking spray and place as many shrimp as you can in an even layer on the CrispLid basket.

3. Place the CrispLid trivet inside the inner steel pot of the cooker and set the fryer basket at the top of the trivet. Then put the CrispLid at the top of the inner steel pot and plug it in. Set the temperature to 500°F and cook for 4 minutes. Repeat the steps until all shrimp are cooked.

4. Place all corn tortillas in a stack in the CrispLid fryer basket. Set to 300°F for 5 minutes. Or, if you like them charred, cook them individually for about 1 minute per side on 500°F.

5. Make a mixture of sour cream, lime juice, and salt together in a bowl until lime crema is smooth.

6. Build tacos with several shrimps, mango, avocado, onion, cilantro, and lime crema.

Nutrition Facts Per Serving

Calories 416 Protein 30g Carbohydrates 33.7g Fat 18g

Spicy Shrimps

Prep Time: 5 minutes, Cook Time: 4 minutes; Serves 4

Ingredients

1 pound shrimp, peeled and deveined

1 tablespoon Cholula hot sauce

1 tablespoon olive oil

2 tsp salt and freshly ground black pepper

cooking spray

Instructions

1. Place shrimp, Cholula, and olive oil in a large bowl and toss to evenly coat the shrimp. Add salt and pepper and then toss it again. Marinate at room temperature for 10 minutes or in the refrigerator for up to 2 hours.

2. Spray CrispLid fryer basket with cooking spray and place as many shrimp as you can in an even layer on the CrispLid basket.

3. Place the CrispLid trivet inside the inner steel pot of the cooker and set the fryer basket at the top of the trivet. Place the CrispLid at the top of the inner steel pot and then plug it in. Cook for another 4 minutes at a temperature of 500°F. Repeat the steps until all the shrimp are cooked.

Nutrition Facts Per Serving

Calories 156 Protein 26g Carbohydrates 1.8g Fat 5g

Chapter 6 Vegan and Vegetables

Green Beans & Artichokes

Prep time: 10 minutes, Cook time: 10 minutes; Serves 8

Ingredients

1 lb trimmed green beans

15 ounces of quartered artichoke

4 tsp butter

1 cup of finely chopped onions

3 minced garlic cloves

½ tsp salt

½ tsp black pepper

1 slice of whole-wheat bread ground into breadcrumbs

⅓ cup finely shredded Romano cheese

Instructions

1. Pour a cup of water in the instant pot.

2. Add green beans and artichokes to the pot's steamer basket and place it on the trivet. Close the lid and let steam for a minute.

3. After a quick release, remove the veggies and drain the water from your pot.

4. Set the pot to sauté and melt 2 tsp butter in it.

5. Toast the breadcrumbs in the melted butter until crisp.

6. Mix it with shredded Romano and your topping is ready.

7. Put the remaining butter in the pot and add some minced garlic and finely chopped onions. Cook until softened.

8. Put the steamed beans and artichokes in the pot along with a pinch of salt and pepper.

9. Add the cheese and breadcrumbs topping to it and cover the pot with Mealthy Crisp lid

10. Set for 3-4 minutes and enjoy it!

Nutrition Facts Per Serving

Calories 59 Carbohydrates 2g Protein 6g Fat 3g

Cauliflower Gnocchi

Prep time: 5 minutes, Cook time: 18 minutes; Serves 2

Ingredients

1 package Trader Joe's cauliflower gnocchi

cooking spray

Instructions

1. Place gnocchi in one layer in the CrispLid fryer basket, working in batches as needed. Coat gnocchi lightly on all sides with cooking spray.

2. Place the CrispLid trivet in the inner steel pot of the cooker. Also, set the fryer basket on top of the trivet.

3. Set the temperature to 400°F and cook for 9 minutes. Flip gnocchi and cook for an additional 9 minutes. Lift the lid and set the dish on the silicone mat.

Nutrition Facts Per Serving

Calories 204 Protein 9g Carbohydrates 37.7g Fat 2g

Pressure Cooker White Rice

Prep time: 15 min, Cook time: 3 min; Serves 1

Ingredients

1 cup long-grain white rice, rinsed*

1/2 teaspoon salt

1 1/4 cups water

Instructions

1. Rinse the rice. Then add water, rice, and salt to the pressure cooker pot.

2. Lock the lid in place. Select 3 minutes timer and put it on high pressure. Turn off the pressure cooker after the timer beeps. Let the pressure in the cooker release naturally. After 10 minutes do a quick pressure release.

3. Serve it hot.

Nutrition Facts Per Serving

Calories 138 Fat 0.2g Carbohydrates 31.3g Protein 2.7g

Crispy Cauliflower

Prep time: 10 minutes, Cook time: 6 minutes; Serves 4

Ingredients

4 cups cauliflower florets

1 tablespoon olive oil

1/2 teaspoon salt

1/4 teaspoon freshly ground black pepper

1 pinch nutmeg (optional)

Instructions

1. Take cauliflower, oil, salt, black pepper, and nutmeg and toss them together in a bowl.

2. Now take the CrispLid fryer basket and place the cauliflower in a single row. Place the CrispLid trivet in the inner steel pot of the cooker and at the top of the trivet, set the fryer basket.

3. Close the Lid and plug it in. Set the temperature to 425°F and cook it for 6 to 8 minutes.

4. Put the crispy cauliflower on a platter and repeat the procedure for the remaining cauliflower.

Nutrition Facts Per Serving

Calories 64 Protein 2g Carbohydrates 5.2g Fat 4g

Artichoke Stuffed Mushrooms

Prep time: 10 minutes, Cook time: 5 minutes; Serves 6

Ingredients

1/2 cup cream cheese, room temperature

1/2 cup chopped artichoke hearts

1/4 cup shredded Parmesan cheese

1 tablespoon lemon juice

1/2 teaspoon kosher salt

1/2 teaspoon garlic powder

1/4 teaspoon freshly ground black pepper

8 Portobello mushrooms, stems and gills removed

1/4 cup panko bread crumbs

cooking spray

Instructions

1. Stir cream cheese, artichoke hearts, Parmesan cheese, lemon juice, salt, garlic powder, and black pepper together in a bowl. Spoon artichoke mixture into each mushroom and top with bread crumbs, pressing to ensure they stick.

2. Spray mushrooms all over with cooking spray and place in a single layer in the CrispLid fryer basket.

3. Place the CrispLid trivet in the inner steel pot of the cooker. Also, set the fryer basket at the top of the trivet.

4. Plug it in the switch. Set to 425°F and cook until mushrooms are browned on the top and cooked through 10 to 12 minutes.

Nutrition Facts Per Serving

Calories 109 Protein 4.2g Carbohydrates 6.5g Fat 7.4g

Fried Okra

Prep time: 15 minutes, Cook time: 8 minutes; Serves 4

Ingredients

1 cup cornmeal

1/4 cup all-purpose flour

50 gm kosher 2 tsp salt to taste

1/2 pound fresh okra, cut into ½-inch slices

1 large egg, beaten

cooking spray

Instructions

1. Combine cornmeal, flour, and salt in a gallon-size resealable plastic bag.

2. Dip okra in egg and transfer to cornmeal mixture. Shake the bag for okra to be coated well.

3. Arrange coated okra to CrispLid fryer basket and spray it with cooking spray. Place the CrispLid trivet in the inner steel pot of pressure cooker and put the fryer basket at top of the trivet.

4. Plug it in the socket after closing the CrispLid. Set the temperature to 400°F and cook okra for 4 minutes. Flip okra using tongs and continue cooking until lightly golden and crispy, about 4 minutes more. Keep flipping the Okra until it becomes crispy and light golden in color. Lift the lid using the handle and set it on the silicone mat. Repeat with remaining okra.

Nutrition Facts Per Serving

Calories 179 Protein 6g Carbohydrates 32.1g Fat 3g

Broccoli Cheddar Quiche

Prep time: 10 minutes, Cook time: 25 minutes; Serves 4

Ingredients

6 eggs

½ cup almond milk/whole milk

1 diced red bell pepper

1 cup finely chopped broccoli

½ cup cheddar cheese

1 cup of water

Olive oil

Instructions

1. Spray your instant pot with olive oil and whisk 6 eggs in it.
2. Add almond milk and whisk thoroughly for a minute.
3. Stir in the chopped broccoli and bell peppers and cook until softens.
4. Sprinkle some cheese and set the mixture aside in an instant-pot-safe dish.
5. Pour a cup of water in the pot and lower the quiche into the pot.
6. Lock the pot with the Mealthy crisp lid and cook for 25 minutes.

Nutrition Facts Per Serving

Calories 189.9 Protein 13.8g Carbohydrates 6g Fat 12.3g

Crustless Zucchini Quiche

Prep time: 10 minutes, Cook time: 20 minutes; Serves 6

Ingredients

2 medium thin-sliced zucchini

1 finely chopped onion

15 ounces of part-skim ricotta

3 eggs

1 cup shredded mozzarella

1 tablespoon butter/olive oil

20 mg black pepper

½ teaspoon dried basil

½ teaspoon dried oregano

olive oil cooking spray

Instructions

1. Set your Instant pot to sauté and add butter or olive oil.

2. Cook the sliced zucchini until it begins to soften.

3. Add chopped onions and cook for 5 more minutes or until tender.

4. Stir in seasoning and pepper and turn off the instant pot.

5. Beat 3 eggs In an instant-pot-safe dish and add ricotta and mozzarella.

6. Fold in the zucchini and onion mixture and set the dish aside.

7. Add a cup of water to the pot and place the trivet at its bottom. Carefully place the dish on the trivet.

8. Lock the lid with Mealthy crisp lid and cook the quiche for 30 minutes.

9. After the cooking time, do a ten-minute natural release.

10. Broil the dish on low to get a crispy top before serving!

Nutrition Facts Per Serving

Calories: 207 Protein: 13.9g Carbohydrates 12.5 Fat 11.3g

Okra & Green Beans

Prep time: 10 minutes, Cook time: 20 minutes; Serves 4

Ingredients

½ bag of frozen cut okra

½ bag of frozen green beans

olive oil spray

¼ cup yeast

salt and pepper to taste

Instructions

1. Pour the frozen okra and green beans into a dish and add water. Cook them for 10 minutes, tossing after every 2 minutes.

2. Once the veggies are back to normal, spray some olive oil on them.

3. Add nutritional yeast, salt, and pepper to the veggies and toss.

4. Place the mixture into your instant pot and cover with a Mealthy crisp lid. Cook for 20 minutes, opening to toss every few minutes.

Nutrition Facts Per Serving

Calories 63 Protein 5g Carbohydrates 2g Fat 3.9g

Stuffed Peppers

Prep time: 20 Min, Cook Time: 23 Min; Serves 4

Ingredients

1 tablespoon vegetable oil

1/4 cup finely chopped red onion

1 tomato, finely chopped

2 teaspoons coriander powder

1/2 teaspoon red chili powder

1/2 teaspoon grounded dried mango

1/2 teaspoon turmeric powder (optional)

1/2 teaspoon ground cumin

1/2 teaspoon garam masala

1 cup boiled potatoes

2 tablespoons green peas (optional)

2 tablespoons corn kernels (optional)

4 green bell peppers

1/4 cup shredded mozzarella cheese (optional)

Instruction

1. Turn the Heat half the oil in a heavy bottom pan over medium heat; add onion. Sauté until onion is softened and turns pink, about 2 minutes.

2. Mix tomato, coriander powder, cumin, turmeric, red chile powder, and amchur into onion. Heat for about 1 minute until tomatoes are cooked through. Put green peas, potatoes, and corn kernels to tomato mixture. Cook for about 2 minutes until potato filling is cooked through.

3. Horizontally chop off the top part of each green bell pepper. Remove the membranes and seeds from inside every bell pepper. Remove small portions of the uneven bell pepper from the bottom to make it stand sturdy. Do not to create an opening at the bottom of the bell pepper.

4. Coat each bell pepper with remaining oil.

5. Divide into 4 equal portions of the potato filling and stuff it inside each bell pepper.

6. Carefully place stuffed bell peppers.

7. Set Mealthy Crisplid to 325°F and cook for about 8-12 minutes until bell peppers are tender.

8. Dredge shredded mozzarella cheese over potato stuffing in bell peppers. Return the CrispLid to the inner steel pot and cook until cheese melts, about 1 minute.

9. Remove the CrispLid and let it cool down.

Nutrition Facts Per Serving

Calories 122 Protein 3g Carbohydrates 14.1g Fat 6g

Hassel back Potatoes

Prep time: 10 min, Cook time: 40 min; Serves 2

Ingredients

2 tablespoons butter, softened

1/2 teaspoon minced garlic

2tsp kosher salt and freshly ground black pepper

2 small gold potatoes

chopped fresh parsley

1 tablespoon olive oil

Instructions

1. Mix garlic, butter, salt, olive oil, and black pepper together in a small bowl.
2. Cut potatoes into thin slices, but leave ¼ inch at the bottom unsliced.
3. Brush half the butter mixture on the potatoes. Make sure all the slices have butter evenly applied.
4. Place potatoes in the CrispLid fryer basket.
5. Set Mealthy CrispLid on top of the inner steel pot and set it to 350°F (180°C). Cook potatoes for 10 minutes and keep flipping potatoes using tongs and continue cooking for 10 minutes more.

Nutrition Facts Per Serving

Calories 312 Protein 4.2g Carbohydrates 31.5g Fat 18.8g

Asparagus

Prep time: 10 min, Cook time: 10 min; Serves 2

Ingredients

1/2 cup Italian-style bread crumbs

1/4 cup all-purpose flour

1/8 teaspoon sea salt

1/2 pound asparagus spears, trimmed

1/8 teaspoon freshly ground black pepper

1 large egg, lightly beaten

cooking spray

Instructions

1. Combine bread crumbs, black pepper, and salt in a shallow bowl. Place flour in a separate shallow bowl.

2. Dredge asparagus spears in flour and shake any excess off also dip spears in egg and allow any excess to drip off.

3. Lightly press the bread crumb mixture to the Dredge asparagus to do the coating.

4. Set the Mealthy CrispLid to 400°F and cook the asparagus for about 5 minutes. Keep flipping the asparagus for another 5 minutes and continue cooking until golden brown.

Nutrition Facts Per Serving

Calories 197 Protein 10g Carbohydrates 30.3g Fat 4g

Eggplant Parmesan

Prep time: 10 min Cook time: 4 min; Serves 2

Ingredients

cooking spray

1 cup tortilla chips

1/4 cup pico de gallo

1/2 cup Mexican cheese blend

1/4 cup black beans

1/4 cup shredded cooked chicken

Instructions

1. Spray CrispLid fryer basket with cooking spray.

2. Layer half the black beans, half the chips, half the pico de gallo, half the chicken, and half the Mexican cheese blend in the Mealthy lid fryer basket. Continue layering with similar ingredients.

3. Set the Mealthy lid to 400°F (200°C) and continue cooking for 4 minutes, until cheese is bubbling and lightly brown.

4. Serve hot!

Nutrition Facts Per Serving

Calories 198 Protein 8g Carbohydrates 28g Fat 6g

Eggplant Fries

Prep Time: 15 minutes, Cook Time: 14 minutes; Serves 4

Ingredients

1 cup panko bread crumbs

3/4 teaspoon kosher salt

1/2 cup all-purpose flour

2 large eggs

1 eggplant, cut into fries

Instructions

1. Take a shallow bowl that is large enough to fit eggplant fries. Combine panko bread crumbs and salt. Pour flour in another shallow bowl of the same size. Taking another shallow bowl of the same size, beat eggs in it.

2. Put the eggplant fries in flour, carefully shake the excess flour back in the bowl. Now dip it in the eggs and wait till the excess drip back to the bowl.

3. Lightly press the eggplant fries in the bread crumbs till they are coated.

4. Now coat the eggplant fries with cooking spray and place them side by side in the CrispLid fryer basket, in separate batches. Place the CrispLid trivet inside the inner steel pot of the cooker and set the fryer basket at the top of the trivet.

5. Plugin CrispLid after setting it on the top of the inner steel pot. Set the temperature at 400°F and cook eggplant for 7 minutes. Flip eggplant fries using tongs and continue cooking until they turn golden brown. Lift the lid using the handle and place it on the silicone mat.

Nutrition Facts Per Serving

Calories 349 Protein 11g Carbohydrates 56g Fat 9g

Kale chips

Prep Time: 5 minutes, Cook Time: 4 minutes; Serves 4

Ingredients

6 cups (1 inch) pieces chopped kale leaves

2 tablespoons olive oil

1 teaspoon garlic powder

1/2 teaspoon salt

1/4 teaspoon onion powder

1/8 teaspoon ground black pepper

Instructions

1. Mix kale and olive oil together in a large bowl until kale is thoroughly coated.

2. Add garlic powder, salt, onion powder, and black pepper to kale and toss until leaves are evenly coated.

3. Arrange kale in a single layer in CrispLid fryer basket, working in batches. Set CrispLid trivet in inner steel pot of pressure cooker and set fryer basket on top of the trivet.

4. Place the CrispLid at the top of the inner steel pot and then plug it in. Set the temperature at 375°F and cook for 6 minutes.

5. Shake fryer basket to move the leaves around. Make sure leaves are evenly distributed.

6. Continue cooking until crispy, about 2 minutes more. Lift the lid using the handle and set it on the silicone mat.

7. Transfer kale chips to a baking sheet to cool without touching each other (or else they will steam and not stay crisp).

8. Repeat with the remaining kale.

9. Enjoy immediately or allow to cool completely. Keep it in an airtight container for 2 days at room temperature.

Nutrition Facts Per Serving

Calories 89 Protein 3g Carbohydrates 8g Fat 5g

Asian Kale Salad with Sweet Pear and Red Crispy Tofu

Prep Time: 10 minutes, Cook Time: 15 minutes; Serves 4

Ingredients

2 tablespoons soy sauce

3 tablespoons rice vinegar

2 teaspoons rice vinegar

1 tablespoon toasted sesame oil

1 tablespoon ginger juice

5 tablespoons vegetable oil

6 large curly kale leaves, ribs removed and finely julienned

1 pound tofu, extra firm packed in water

2 teaspoons gochujang (Korean chili-bean paste)

2 teaspoons honey

2 teaspoons rice vinegar

1 ripe Anjou or Asian pear - halved, peeled, and sliced into 1/4-inch wedges

Instructions

1. Whisk together soy sauce, vinegar, sesame oil, ginger juice and 2 tablespoons vegetable oil. Toss kale and let stand; about 20 minutes; transfer to a serving platter.

2. Heat remaining vegetable oil in a large nonstick skillet over medium-high heat and fry tofu, turning the pieces until crispy on all sides, 5 to 7 minutes; transfer to a paper towel-lined plate.

3. Stir together gochujang, honey, and remaining rice vinegar in a medium-sized bowl. Add crispy tofu; toss and coat.

4. Garnish kale salad with pear slices and crispy tofu to serve.

Nutrition Facts Per Serving

Calories 452 Protein 19g Carbohydrates 26.6g Fat 30g

Chapter 7 Beef, Lamb, and Pork

Beef & Cauliflower Cheeseburger Mac

Prep time: 15 minutes, Cook time: 15 minutes; Serves 4

Ingredients

1 lb lean grass ground beef

1 small to medium cauliflower

4 tsp rice flour/almond flour

4 tsp butter/ vegan butter

1 cup of unsweetened almond milk/milk of your choice

2 cups of shredded cheddar

2 tsp Himalayan Salt

Instructions

1. Place the head of cauliflower on the trivet of an instant cooker and add a cup of water.

2. Set to steam for a minute.

3. Release right away and carefully remove the cauliflower. Cut it into little pieces and set aside.

4. Drain the water from the pot and set it to sauté.

5. Add 1 lb of ground beef to the pot and cook until it's brown. Set aside with the cauliflowers

6. Add 4 tsp of butter to your instant pot and let it melt.

7. Whisk 4 tsp of rice flour in the melted butter until it forms an even mixture.

8. Add a cup of almond milk whisk until mixture begins to thicken.

9. Once thickened, stir in a cup of cheddar and add a pinch of Himalayan salt.

10. Once the cheese melts, add beef and cauliflower and mix well.

11. Top it with the remaining cheese and cover the pot with Mealthy crisp lid.

12. Set for 2-3 minutes.

Nutrition Facts Per Serving

Calories 381 Protein 14g Carbohydrates 10.2g Fat 31.6g

Easy Chicken Breast

Prep time: 5 min, Cook time: 20min; Serves 2

Ingredients

2 (6 ounce) boneless, skinless chicken breasts

cooking spray

1/4 teaspoon garlic powder (optional)

1/8 teaspoon ground black pepper (optional)

1/4 teaspoon salt

Instructions

1. Spray cooking spray on chicken breasts and Mealthy Crisplid fryer basket.

2. Season chicken with salt, garlic powder, and black pepper.

3. Place coated chicken breasts in one layer in the fryer basket, working in batches if needed.

4. Set the Mealthy CrispLid to 350°F and cook chicken for 20-24 minutes until a nearby inserted thermometer reads at least 165°F

5. Serve hot and spicy!

Nutrition Facts Per Serving

Calories 186 Fat 4g Carbohydrates 0.4g Protein 37g

Meatloaf & Mashed Potatoes

Prep time: 10 minutes; Cook time: 30 minutes; Serves 6

Ingredients

2 lb lean ground beef

¼ cup of seasoned breadcrumbs

¼ cup diced onion

4 cloves of minced garlic

3 cloves of whole garlic

1 egg

1 cup shredded pecorino Romano cheese

1 tsp dry parsley/1 tablespoon freshly chopped parsley

18 ounces canned tomato sauce

3 cups peeled golden potatoes (quartered)

3 cups baby carrots

3 tablespoon butter

1 cup of chicken broth/chicken stock

2tsp Salt and pepper

Instructions

1. In your instant pot, place the quartered potatoes, 3 cloves of whole garlic, and 1 tsp salt.

2. Pour in a cup of chicken broth and place the trivet on top of the potatoes.

3. Lay tin foil down on the trivet and place baby carrots on top of the foil. Add 1 tablespoon butter and cover with another piece of foil.

4. Add breadcrumbs, onion, minced garlic, 2 tablespoon tomato sauce, an egg, cheese, and parsley to the minced beef and mix well.

5. Shape the mixture into a circular loaf and put the loaf on top of the carrot layer.

6. Pour 4 tablespoons of tomato sauce on top of the meatloaf and cover the pot with Mealthy Crisp Lid. Lock and cook for 25 minutes.

7. After all the steam unlocks, remove the meatloaf and carrots from the pot.

8. Drain the potatoes and reserve the broth.

9. Mash the potatoes and add in broth 2 tablespoons of butter. To make it extra creamy, add a splash of milk/Greek yogurt.

10. Season salt and pepper to taste and Enjoy.

Nutrition Facts Per Serving

Calories 468 Proteins 52.4g Carbohydrates 25.3 Fat 17.5g

Cauliflower Mash with Bacon

Prep time: 5 minutes, Cook time: 15 minutes; Serves 4

Ingredients

8 slices of diced bacon

1 cauliflower head (chopped or broken apart)

2 tablespoon parmesan cheese

4 tsp butter

¼ tsp salt

Freshly chopped chives

⅔ cup cheddar

1 cup chicken broth/water

Instructions

1. Set your instant pot on sauté and spray some cooking oil.

2. Sauté diced bacon until they turn crispy. Remove in a dish and set aside.

3. Add a cup of chicken broth or water to the pot and set the cauliflower in a steam basket.

4. Lock the lid and steam for 3 minutes.

5. Do a quick release after the cooking time.

6. Place the cauliflower in a food processor and add 2 tsp butter, 2 tsp parmesan cheese and a pinch of salt. Pulse until creamy.

7. Place the mashed cauliflower in an instant-pot-safe dish and top with shredded cheddar and bacon.

8. Put the dish into your pot and cover with Mealthy Crisp Lid. Broil until the cheese is golden-brown and bubbly.

9. Garnish with freshly chopped chives and enjoy!

Nutrition Facts Per Serving

Calories 94 Carbohydrates 3g Protein 7g Fat 6g

Baked Ziti

Prep time: 10 minutes, Cook time: 2 minutes; Serves 6

Ingredients

1 lb lean ground beef

½ diced onion

2 tsp olive oil

3 cloves of minced garlic

1 tsp Himalayan salt

½ cup of water

2 ½ cups of gluten-free pasta

28 ounces of crushed tomatoes

2 T fresh basil/1 tsp dried basil

1 tsp oregano

2 cups of finely chopped spinach

¾ cup ricotta cheese

1 cup shredded mozzarella

⅓ cup Romano Cheese

Instructions

1. Set your instant pot to sauté and add 2 tsp olive oil.

2. Add in meat and cook until brown.

3. Add diced onions and cook until the onions get tender.

4. If necessary, drain the meat and then add 1 tsp olive oil and minced garlic. Cook until garlic is fragrant and sprinkle a pinch of salt.

5. Add a cup of water to the pot and scrape off brown bits at its bottom with a wooden spoon.

6. Layer the uncooked pasta over the meat mixture.

7. Mix some basil and oregano into crushed tomatoes and layer it over the pasta. Do not stir!

8. Cover the pot with Mealthy Crisp Lid and cook for 2 minutes. For Banza pasta, cook for 3 minutes

9. After this, do a quick release.

10. Stir everything well and add chopped spinach.

11. Allow the spinach to wilt before stirring in ricotta and mozzarella cheese. Broil the cheese until it's brown and bubbly and enjoy.

Nutrition Facts Per Serving

Calories 1393 Protein 66.2g Carbohydrates 144g Fat 61.4g

Pot Pork Ribs

Prep Time: 15 min, Cook Time: 45 min; Serves 4

Ingredients

1 1/2- 2lbs rack baby back ribs

1/2 teaspoon liquid smoke optional

1 cup broth or water

1 onion sliced

6 tablespoons dry rub

4 cloves garlic sliced

10 ml barbecue sauce (optional)

Instructions

1. Rinse ribs and pat dry. Clean it properly. Remove the thin ribs membrane.

2. Cut the slab into 2-3 pieces and coat with dry rub massaging it into the meat.

3. Place trivet in the bottom. Add broth or liquid smoke if using.

4. Sprinkle onion and garlic over the ribs. Set it upright for better application.

5. Close the Mealthy lid and select manual pressure. Set the timer for 23 minutes approximately. Once the timer buzzes, allow the pot to naturally release for 5 minutes.

6. You can also open the valve to release the remaining pressure.

7. Brush the dish with barbecue sauce (or olive oil/salt/pepper for dry ribs) and broil or grill until slightly charred.

Nutrition Facts Per Serving

Calories 212 Protein 7.4g Carbohydrates 3.3g Fat 18.8g

Buffalo Wings

Prep Time: 5 min; Cook Time: 29 min; Serves 8

Ingredients

cooking spray

1 teaspoon garlic powder

1/2 cup Buffalo wing sauce

2 pounds chicken wings

1 teaspoon kosher salt

Instructions

1. Place CrispLid trivet in inner steel pot of pressure cooker. Set Mealthy CrispLid to 375°F (190°C) to preheat. Spray the fryer basket with cooking spray.

2. Use a clean paper towel to dry pat chicken wings and season with salt and garlic powder.

3. Working in batches, place seasoned chicken wings in a single layer in greased fryer basket and place the basket in the inner steel pot of pressure cooker.

4. Cook wings for 15 minutes; flip wings and continue cooking for 10 minutes more.

5. Increase heat to 450°F (200°C) and cook for 2 minutes; flip and cook for another 2 minutes. Make sure that the thermometer inserted near the bone should read at least 165°F (75°C).

Nutrition Facts Per Serving

Calories 209 Protein 32.9g Carbohydrates 0.3g Fat 8.5g

Asian Beef Lead

Prep time: 10 min, Cook time: 10 min; Serves 2

Ingredients

1/4 cup soy sauce

1 tablespoon Sriracha hot sauce

1 teaspoon garlic powder

1 teaspoon ground ginger

1 1/2 teaspoons sesame oil

1 1/2 teaspoons brown sugar

1/2 pound beef hanger steak

cooking spray

Instructions

1. Place Sriracha sauce, sesame oil, soy sauce, brown sugar, garlic powder, and ground ginger in a gallon-size resealable bag. Shake it well to combine. Remove all the air and leave just a single steak in the bag. Marinate it for 30 minutes to 48 hours.

2. Spray the dry steak, with cooking spray and place gently in the CrispLid fryer basket.

3. Set the Mealthy crisp Lid to 500°F and cook for 5 minutes. Flip and cook for another 5 minutes for medium-rare. The internal temperature should read 145°F (63°C).

4. Place the transfer steak to a cutting board to rest for 10 minutes. Chop the steak evenly and thinly against the grain.

Nutrition Facts Per Serving

Calories 389 Protein 33g Carbohydrates 8g Fat 25g

Healthy Bacon

Prep time: 5 min, Cook time: 9 min; Serves 2

Ingredients

1/3 pound thick-cut bacon

Instructions

1. Pour ½ inch water into the steel pot of pressure cooker.

2. Cut bacon into smaller pieces so that it is easy to cook and also can fit into the Mealthy Crisplid fryer basket without overlapping. Try to place without overlapping.

3. Set Mealthy CrispLid to 350°F and cook bacon for about 9 minutes, until crispy.

Nutrition Facts Per Serving

Calories 339 Protein 25g Carbohydrates 1.3g Fat 26g

Beef Empanadas

Prep Time: 20 minutes, Cook Time: 15 minutes; Serves 8

Ingredients

1 package puff pastry

1 tablespoon canola oil

1/4 pound lean ground beef

1/4 cup chopped white onion

1/4 cup chopped red bell pepper

1 teaspoon ground cumin

1/2 teaspoon sweet paprika

1/4 teaspoon dried oregano

2 tsp kosher salt and freshly ground black pepper

1 egg

1 tablespoon water

Cooking spray

Instructions

1. Let puff pastry dough sit for 15 minutes at room temperature.

2. Heat oil in a skillet over medium-high. Add beef and onion; cook and stir, breaking ground beef into crumbles, until starting to brown, about 3 minutes. Add red bell pepper; cook, stirring occasionally until red bell pepper is starting to soften, about 4 minutes. Season ground beef mixture with cumin, paprika, oregano, salt, and ground black pepper. Drain oil and transfer ground beef filling to a bowl; let cool 5 minutes.

3. Cut the puff pastry into rounds, about 6 inches in diameter.

4. Place 1 to 2 tablespoons filling in the center of each puff pastry round. Brush it with water around half of the outer edge of each round. Fold them over the filling and then seal the edges by pinching by using a fork, crimp edges. Repeat process with remaining wrappers and filling.

5. Form an egg wash by mixing one egg with a tablespoon of water in a bowl. Brush each empanada with egg wash and spray with cooking spray. Arrange empanadas in the CrispLid fryer basket in a single layer, working in batches as needed.

6. Place the CrispLid at the top of the inner steel pot and plug it in. Set the temperature to 400°F and cook it for 4 minutes. Flip empanadas using tongs and continue cooking until light golden brown, about 4 minutes. Repeat with remaining empanadas. Lift the lid using the handle and set it on the silicone mat.

Nutrition Facts Per Serving

Calories 74 Protein 5.4g Carbohydrates 2.6g Fat 4.7g

Kheema Meatloaf (Lamb Meatloaf)

Prep Time: 5 minutes, Cook Time: 4 minutes; Serves 4

Ingredients

Cooking spray

1 pound ground lamb

2 eggs, lightly beaten

1 cup diced yellow onions

1/4 cup chopped fresh cilantro

1 tablespoon minced fresh ginger

1 tablespoon minced garlic

2 teaspoons garam masala, or more to taste

1 teaspoon salt

1 teaspoon ground turmeric

1 teaspoon cayenne pepper

1/2 teaspoon ground cinnamon

1/8 teaspoon ground cardamom

Instructions

1. Place the CrispLid trivet inside the inner steel pot of the cooker and set the fryer basket at the top of the trivet. Add 1½ cups water to the inner steel pot.

2. Cut a 12-inch square sheet of aluminum foil. Spray cooking spray onto the foil.

3. Mix ground lamb, eggs, onion, cilantro, ginger, garlic, garam masala, salt, turmeric, cayenne, cinnamon, and cardamom in a bowl until thoroughly combined.

4. Form lamb mixture into a round loaf, and place onto the foil. Pull corners and sides of foil up, and cover loaf very loosely. Place the covered loaf onto the fryer basket.

5. Lock the cooker lid and then set steam vent to Sealing. Select the Pressure Cook (Manual) and cook it for 20 minutes on High Pressure. When the pressure releases after 10 minutes, then set a steam vent handle to Venting to quick-release remaining pressure.

6. Open the foil packet and lay the foil flat. Allow any liquid and Fat to drain off. Unplug pressure cooker.

7. Place the CrispLid at the top of the inner steel pot and then plug it in. Set the temperature at 400°F and then cook further for the next 4 minutes. Cook for another 4 minutes and flip the meatloaf till the edges are crispy and brown in color. A thermometer placed inside should read the temperature of 160°F.

8. Drain Fat and liquid and let stand 5 minutes before slicing.

Nutrition Facts Per Serving

Calories 387 Protein 32g Carbohydrates 8.7g Fat 25g

Pork Chops

Prep Time: 10 minutes, Cook Time: 15 minutes; Serves 4

Ingredients

6 (5 ounces) center-cut boneless pork chops, Fat trimmed

1/2 teaspoon fine sea salt

1/2 cup panko bread crumbs

1/3 cup crushed cornflakes cereal

1/2 teaspoon garlic powder

1/2 teaspoon onion powder

1/4 teaspoon paprika

2 mg freshly ground black pepper to taste

1 large egg

cooking spray

Instructions

1. Season pork chops on both sides with sea salt. Set aside.

2. Combine panko bread crumbs, crushed cornflakes cereal, garlic powder, onion powder, paprika, and black pepper in a shallow bowl. Beat egg in a separate shallow bowl.

3. Dip pork chop into beaten egg, allowing any excess to drip off. Dredge chops in the bread crumb mixture, gently pressing to fully coat.

4. Place 2 to 3 pork chops in CrispLid fryer basket and generously spray with cooking spray.

5. Place CrispLid trivet in inner steel pot of pressure cooker and set fryer basket on the trivet.

6. Place the CrispLid at the top of the inner steel pot and then plug it in. Set CrispLid to 400°F and cook for 10 minutes. Flip pork chops and continue cooking until crispy on the outside and a thermometer inserted near the center reads at least 145°F, 5 to 10 minutes more.

7. Repeat with remaining chops.

Nutrition Facts Per Serving

Calories 387 Protein 32g Carbohydrates 8.7g Fat 25g

Steak Tacos

Prep Time: 10 minutes, Cook Time: 18 minutes; Serves 4

Ingredients

Steak:

1 pound hanger steak

2 tsp salt and ground black pepper to taste

5 limes, juiced

1/4 cup olive oil

cooking spray

5 ml Spicy Crema:

1/4 cup sour cream

1 tablespoon Cholula hot sauce (or any hot sauce), or more to taste

1/2 lime, juiced

8 small flour tortillas

Instructions

1. Season steak with salt and black pepper. Put it in a plastic bag and add juice from 5 limes and olive oil. Marinate it for the next 30 minutes but no longer or the steak will start to break down.

2. Remove the steak and then pat dry it; season with more salt and black pepper. Spray steak with cooking spray and place in CrispLid fryer basket.

3. Place the CrispLid trivet inside the inner steel pot of the cooker and set the fryer basket at the top of the trivet.

4. Place the CrispLid at the top of the inner steel pot and then plug it in. Set the temperature to 500°F and cook for 5 minutes, then flip and cook for 5 additional minutes for medium-rare. Give a 10 minutes rest to steak by placing it on a plate or the cutting board.

5. Stir sour cream, Cholula hot sauce, the juice from ½ lime, and salt together in a small bowl until spicy crema is evenly combined.

6. Place CrispLid trivet in the inner steel pot of pressure cooker. Spray over the tortillas lightly on both sides with cooking spray. Set 1 tortilla onto the trivet in the pressure cooker.

7. Place the CrispLid at the top of the inner steel pot and then plug it in. Set the temperature to 450°F and cook for 30 seconds per side. Repeat with remaining tortillas.

8. Slice steak thinly against the grain.

9. Arrange steak onto each tortilla and top with spicy crema.

Nutrition Facts Per Serving

Calories 339 Protein 25g Carbohydrates 1.3g Fat 26g

Chapter 8 Desserts

Banana Bread

Prep time: 15 minutes, Cook time: 30 minutes; Serves 8

Ingredients

Cooking spray

3/4 cup all-purpose flour

1 teaspoon ground cinnamon

1/2 teaspoon kosher salt

1/4 teaspoon baking soda

2 bananas, mashed

2 large eggs, beaten

1/2 cup white sugar

1/4 cup whole milk

2 tablespoons vegetable oil

1/2 teaspoon vanilla extract

2 tablespoons chopped walnuts

Instructions

1. Coat bottom and sides of a 6-inch round cake pan with cooking spray.

2. Whisk flour, cinnamon, salt, and baking soda together in a bowl.

3. Combine bananas, eggs, sugar, milk, oil, and vanilla extract in a separate container.

4. Add the banana mixture into flour mixture just until batter is combined; pour into prepared cake pan. Sprinkle walnuts over batter.

5. Place trivet in inner steel pot of pressure cooker and set the pan with batter on the trivet.

6. Place the CrispLid at the top of the inner steel pot and then plug-in. Set CrispLid to 325°F and cook until a toothpick comes out clean when inserted in the middle, about 30 minutes.

7. Cool the prepared meal in a pan for 15 minutes. Remove bread from pan to serve.

Nutrition Facts Per Serving

Calories 186 Protein 4g Carbohydrates 29.2g Fat 6g

Apple Crisp

Prep time: 10 minutes, Cook time: 10 minutes; Serves 4

Ingredients

4 cups of diced apples

4 tsp honey/maple syrup

2 tsp cinnamon

1 tsp lemon juice

½ tsp lemon zest

⅔ cup Oats

⅓ cup Almond Flour

9 chopped pecans

¼ tsp salt

4 tsp melted coconut oil

3 tablespoon coconut cream

½ tsp vanilla

Instructions

1. Mix 2 tsp honey, 2tsp cinnamon, ½ tsp lemon zest and 1 tsp lemon juice with diced apples and set aside.

2. Whisk 2 tsp honey with the melted coconut oil for the topping.

3. Stir in the oats, pecans, almond flour, cinnamon, and salt in the honey and coconut oil mixture.

4. Place the diced apples in an instant-pot-safe dish and top evenly with the crisp topping.

5. Add a cup of water to the steel insert of your instant pot and lay the dish on the trivet. In case you want to cook the apple in the inner steel pot, add ½ cup of water to the pot and then topped apples.

6. Cover the pot with Mealthy Crisp Lid and cook for 7 minutes.

7. Safely remove the dish from the pot and place it on a cookie sheet.

8. Let the Apple Crisp cool for about 10 minutes.

9. Mix the coconut cream, honey, and vanilla together and drizzle evenly over the apple crisp.

Nutrition Facts Per Serving

Calories 521 Protein 8.1g Carbohydrates: 52.7 Fat 30.9g

Strawberry Rhubarb Crisp

Prep time: 10 minutes, Cook time: 5 minutes; Serves 4

Ingredients

2 cups diced rhubarb

4 cups diced strawberries

3 ½ tablespoons honey/maple syrup

4 tsp melted coconut oil

⅔ cup of oats

⅓ cup fine almond flour

½ tsp cinnamon

¼ tsp salt

Instructions

1. Toss rhubarb and berries in a medium bowl, with 1 ½ tablespoon of maple syrup.

2. Pour the mixture in an instant-pot-safe dish.

3. For the topping, whisk honey/maple syrup and melted coconut oil in a separate bowl.

4. Add oats, almond flour, cinnamon, and salt to the mixture and stir well.

5. Place the topping over strawberry and rhubarb mixture.

6. Add a cup of water to the steel insert of your instant pot and then insert the trivet.

7. Lay the rhubarb and berry dish on top of the trivet.

8. Cover the pot with a Mealthy crisp lid and cook for 5 minutes.

9. Meanwhile, preheat oven to broil.

10. Remove the dish from the instant pot and place it on a cookie sheet under the broiler.

11. Broil until the crisp topping starts to brown.

12. Let the Crisp sit for 10 minutes before eating.

Nutrition Facts Per Serving

Calories 307 Protein3.8g Carbohydrates 35.5 Fat 16.7g